Male Mythologies

Male Mythologies
John Fowles and Masculinity

Bruce Woodcock

Lecturer in English
University of Hull

THE HARVESTER PRESS · SUSSEX
BARNES & NOBLE BOOKS · NEW JERSEY

First published in Great Britain in 1984 by
THE HARVESTER PRESS LIMITED
Publisher: John Spiers
16 Ship Street, Brighton, Sussex

and in the USA by
BARNES & NOBLE BOOKS
81 Adams Drive, Totowa, New Jersey 07512

© Bruce Woodcock, 1984

British Library Cataloguing in Publication Data

Woodcock, Bruce
    Male mythologies
    1. Fowles, John—Criticism and interpretation
    I. Title   .
    823'.914   PR6056.085Z/

    ISBN 0-7108-0622-1

BARNES & NOBLE BOOKS
ISBN 0-389-20497-8

Photoset in 11/12pt Baskerville by Witwell Ltd., Liverpool.
Printed in Great Britain by
Whitstable Litho Ltd., Whitstable, Kent

Contents

Preface

I am grateful to the following for their permission to use copyright material: Anthony Sheil Associates Ltd, for permission to quote from the works of John Fowles; London Weekend Television, for permission to use the 'South Bank Show' interview and for their help in making the transcript available; The British Broadcasting Corporation for permission to use the BBC2 'Frank Delaney' programme; *New Socialist*, for permission to quote from Sarah Benton's interview.

I would also like to thank all the people who have helped in any way to shape the ideas and material in this book, in particular Les Garry for her patience and encouragement.

The following abbreviations are used throughout in reference to John Fowles's main works. Full details are given in the bibliography.

> *The Aristos—A*
> *The Collector—C*
> *The Magus—M*
> *The Magus—A Revised Version—MRV*
> *The French Lieutenant's Woman—FLW*
> *The Ebony Tower—ET*
> *Daniel Martin—DM*
> *Mantissa—Mt*

1

John Fowles and the masculinity myth

The potency of women's intervention in the sexual arena
lies in the possibility of shedding the whole mythology of
masculinity and femininity.

(Bea Campbell)[1]

'But what's wrong with that man?'

(George Seferis, quoted in *Daniel Martin*)[2]

Masculinity is increasingly being posed as a crucial problem within
western society. Whereas much attention has been given to the
construction of 'femininity', it is only comparatively recently that
the focus has shifted to consider the social construction of
masculinity. This shift is occurring under the influence of two
interrelated factors—a growing sense of crisis among different
groups of men, often for diverse reasons, in the face of advanced
capitalism, and the challenges posed by feminism to the edifice and
power of patriarchy. What is being revealed is obvious—that
sexuality and sexual power never were 'the problem of women' as
such, though analysts have often tended to frame the issues in terms
of women. The *problem* is men, what men are, how they behave, how
they are constructed as men, and the ways in which they inherit,
uphold and propagate the legacy of patriarchy, their own power.[3]

The biggest obstacle to any progressive change in social relations
is quite clearly men themselves, as individuals and as a social class or
power group. Feminists have variously identified war, violence,
competitiveness, distorted sexuality and social exploitation as the
products of patriarchy in itself, or of patriarchy in its capitalistic
form. Such features in society have been seen as specifically 'male',

7

deriving from an ideology within which men are constructed *as* men. But it is only recently that men themselves have begun to analyse and challenge their own power, values and behaviour from within the experience of masculinity.

Inevitably, there are serious contradictions involved in that activity, and we can examine the nature of them through the work of male writers who ask such questions. John Fowles provides a case in point. By looking at Fowles's writing about men, not only is an analysis of contemporary masculinity possible, but the very problems of undertaking such an analysis are themselves laid bare.

Fowles is notable in that he was tackling these issues from the start of his writing career in the 1950s; and, increasingly aware of the contradictions, he has sought out ways of posing himself, as a male writer and fantasist, as part of the very problem under investigation. Whereas some male analysts of masculinity see changing men as something of a cosmetic exercise involving simply changing the social roles men perform, Fowles recognised from the beginning that the crucial issue was male power and control—the power of men over women, and the control of patriarchal social forms over the identities of both. What Fowles presents and analyses through the male characters in his novels is the social legacy of patriarchal ideology and power as lived by the individual man. His fiction implies the need for structural changes in society in order to break the hold of male power. Yet, while his work allows such an analysis to be made, its outcome is an evasion of this central issue, which promotes a realigned version of the very myths of masculinity he lays bare.

This contradiction is central to a critical formulation of the problems involved when men analyse masculinity. Fowles epitomises a condition prevalent among contemporary men who align themselves with feminism. As well as the difficulties of analysing masculinity from within its experience, his case brings out the ambiguous nature of such an alignment and allows us to ask whether it is necessarily ambiguous.

There are a number of preliminary questions to consider, however, before taking Fowles up as a specific case. One question is whether to distinguish an *ideology* of masculinity, or whether instead to talk of masculinity as *part* of ideology in general. We can

8

speak of male roles and of male power with a degree of certainty as to what is being indicated. But any attempt to distinguish 'an ideology of masculinity', or provide a definable model for it, can have the effect of schematising complex and particular social processes, or of suggesting that masculinity is somehow unitary in character. Our presumption needs to be that there is no fixed, homogeneous or transhistorical form of masculinity. Instead, there are changing versions of the gender identity which socially discriminates men from women. Andrew Tolson, one of the earliest of the recent wave of male writers questioning male experience, puts it like this: 'There is no "universal" masculinity, but rather a varying masculine experience of each succeeding social epoch'; 'masculinity has a historical development and is continually re-adapted to new social relations.'[4] 'Men', 'male' and 'masculine' are changing social categories, defined in particular ways to accommodate the demands of particular societies at specific stages of their history. It is into these categories that a newly born infant can be inserted and within them that it can be psychologically and emotionally 'constructed' as a 'man'—*if* it has the decisive emblem of power which, according to the codes of patriarchy, allows both entry into the privileged group and the inheritance of the patriarchal legacy, the penis.

That inheritance in itself is a critically ambiguous experience in the process of becoming 'male'. For the legacy of that power is both a privileging and a restriction, a prescription which by definition proscribes whole areas of human experience as part of the process of social regulation. This is epitomised by the problematic allegiance demanded by the father, as a result of which, to use Tolson's words, masculinity 'is structured in *ambivalence*'.[5] The father in recent Western society is often an alien figure of authority, distanced from the inclusiveness of the mother–child relation. At the same time, for the son he is the promise of a future offering power, equivalence and acceptance, if the son accepts his own identity within the male sphere and aligns himself with its codes. The father affirms masculine power in a double-edged way: the son suffers from that power, the power of denial, restriction, castration, the patriarchal 'no'; and at the same time, the son foresees in the father a future when he himself might act that role. Masculinity, then, is both threatening and mysteriously attractive. Tolson sees it as 'a permanent emotional tension that the individual man must, in some way, strive to overcome', and it is this, in his view, which accounts for the competitiveness of male cultures—a need for recognition, reward and acceptance by a hierarchically structured male peer group which reproduces itself in social institutions through schools and careers: 'what remains hidden in the masculine character, is the emotional insecurity, the ambivalent identification, that started the process in the first place.'[6]

Such views of masculinity, then, present the categories of 'man', 'male', 'masculine' as social constructions, necessarily shaped by and subject to the activities of historical change. The shifting relations of societies demand realignments of power within which 'men' adapt their own self-definitions in order to maintain their hegemony, and the inheritance of that power itself is a problematic one. All this suggests that 'male power' cannot be seen as simple or single. Jeffrey Weeks, another notable recent British analyst of masculinity, summarises the French philosopher Foucault as saying that power 'is not a single thing: it is relational, it is created in the relationships which sustain it'.[7] In that sense, male power is not constituted monolithically as a single locatable entity; nor does it necessarily act coherently for an all-embracing or clearly defined social group which benefits in unchallenged or clear-cut ways. If there are historically contradictory and changing elements in the notion of masculinity, there are accompanying contradictions within the notion of male power itself. Male power both allows and disallows, but unequally across the social classes. Like femininity, masculinity is restrictive in its effects; but crucially, unlike femininity, the very restrictions of masculinity adhere in the 'benefits' of its power to which the individual male accedes. We can talk of 'male mythologies' in the sense that mythologies are the myths of ideology at work within history for the perpetuation of power by a dominant social group under the continuing imperative to assert and maintain its prerogatives. But the notion of myth should not belie the social hold and efficacy of the varying definitions of masculinity. The usefulness of the term lies in its suggestion that such definitions are themselves 'fictional' constructions with a remarkable power to shape the social imagination, but capable of deconstruction.

John Fowles understands masculinity in precisely this way. For him, the myths that contemporary men impose on themselves in their perpetuation of power have a historical root in the legacy of Victorian England. The ideological inheritance of Victorian patriarchy was a set of sexual precepts, handed down and psychologically inscribed through the family, the father and various institutions such as schools, military service and so on. Fowles gives little space in his work to the role of the father in this process, though *Daniel Martin* allows some insights. He tends in general merely to sketch in the early lives of his male characters, preferring instead to focus on male experience at work in the formed individual. But *The French Lieutenant's Woman* investigates that moment of high Victorianism when definitions of masculinity were being formulated which have since shaped the twentieth-century experience represented by the male characters in his other fictions. Moreover, his personal experience as a man comes out of that very ideological legacy, a background which helps explain some of the contradictions in his thinking about what he has called the 'appalling crust' of masculinity.[8]

Fowles's awareness of male power stems in part from his life at public school and during military service. Both of these he now sees as imposing an 'especially rigid' form of masculinity.[9] As head boy at Bedford School, he learnt personally and quite explicitly the nature and effects of male power. By all accounts he enjoyed public school, and when invited to become head boy he could not resist: 'I was totally brainwashed. Little English boys were taught that serving King and Empire—and all that rubbish—was the only true goal in life.'[10] Elsewhere he recalls that

Being head boy was a weird experience. You had total power over 800 other boys; you were totally responsible for discipline and punishment. I spent my 18th year holding court really. I'd have 20 boys before me every morning, who you were both prosecutor and judge of. . . and executioner, of course. I suppose I used to beat on average three or four boys a day. . . Very evil, I think. Terrible system.[11]

He has described his role as 'chief of a Gestapo-like network of prefects', and adds that though 'only half of me believed in this

11

beastly system', it was a 'fortunate experience' since, by the age of 18, he had 'learnt all about power, hierarchy and the manipulation of law. Ever since then I have had a violent hatred of leaders, organisers, bosses: of anyone who thinks it good to get or have arbitrary power over other people.'[12] He has also admitted that since then he has 'always found it difficult to get on with men unless one's in a power situation'.[13]

What his time at public school and in the Royal Marines gave Fowles was an initiation into the realities of male experience in one heightened contemporary form. What it left him with was a deep resentment of it, which sharpened into a critical awareness of the contradictory nature of masculinity. But his very upbringing also marked him as subject to those very contradictions. If in his fictions, at one remove and only just one step ahead, he probes the myths that he sees men as suffering from, his writings and comments on masculinity in general display the difficulties he has in stepping out of his male viewpoint. Even when he analyses male power most directly, he does so in ways which perpetuate some of masculinity's most tenacious myths.

An early example of the contradictions in his thinking can be found in *The Aristos*. Written largely between 1947 and 1950 whilst Fowles was an undergraduate at Oxford,[14] it is a book which Fowles has described both as 'very arrogant'[15] and 'mildly prophetic',[16] admitting that 'there are things in it which I still feel and believe.'[17] In fact, *The Aristos* presents a key ambiguity in his views on male and female roles. Whilst his notion of masculinity as a 'crust' implies that gender is an imposed coating of social conditioning, *The Aristos* proposes a view of masculine and feminine as archetypal principles which contradicts seeing gender as constructed through the social process. Furthermore, though Fowles registers his deep sense of male power as at the root of what is wrong with modern society, the lever for his analysis is an idealisation of the feminine and the female which itself remains unquestioned.

The section called 'Adam and Eve' argues that 'The male and female are the two most powerful biological principles; and their smooth inter-action in society is one of the chief signs of social health.' (*A*, p.157) Our world shows 'considerable sickness' in this respect despite 'the now general political emancipation of

12

women... and most of this sickness arises from the selfish tyranny of the male.' Symptomatically, this view of male and female as biological principles co-exists ambiguously with his explicit support for women as 'progressive' by contrast with the conservative male. The male or 'Adam' principle is defined as 'hatred of change and futile nostalgia for the innocence of animals', while 'Eve is the assumption of human responsibility, of the need for progress and the need to control progress'. Fowles's model of masculinity is nothing if not representative of the schematic stereotyping of patriarchal orthodoxy:

> Adam is stasis, or conservatism; Eve is kinesis, or progress. Adam societies are ones in which the man and the father, male gods, exact strict obedience to established institutions and norms of behaviour, as during a majority of the periods of history in our era. The Victorian is a typical such period. Eve societies are those in which the woman and the mother, female gods, encourage innovation and experiment, and fresh definitions, aims, modes of feeling. The Renaissance and our own are typical such ages. (*A*, p.157)

Yet it is from this 'brew of myths and genes', as Sarah Benton has described it in a recent interview with Fowles,[18] that he launches his critique of male power:

> The petty, cruel and still prevalent antifeminism of Adam-dominated mankind (the very term '*man*kind' is revealing) is the long afterglow of the male's once important physical superiority and greater utility in the battle for survival. To the Adam in man, woman is no more than a rapable receptacle. This male association of femininity with rapability extends far beyond the female body. Progress and innovation are rapable; anything not based on brute power is rapable. All progressive philosophies are feminist. Adam is a princeling in a mountain castle; raids and fortifications, his own power and his own prestige, obsess him. (*A*, p.158)

Fowles captures the contradiction that male power is both an appropriation and a defence mechanism sheltering an insecure ego. Against this, 'the female principle—tolerance, a general scepticism towards the Adam belief that might is right' is the most valuable element in society. Predictably, Fowles elevates motherhood as 'the most fundamental of all trainings in tolerance; and tolerance, as we have still to learn, is the most fundamental of all human wisdoms'.

If this formulation of the problem of male power itself is quite remarkable for its time, the way in which it is framed in terms of female values as a salvation remains thoroughly orthodox. Despite a degree of increasing self-awareness about this contradiction, Fowles continues to be caught up in it. As such he exemplifies certain aspects of the contemporary male position in relation to feminism itself. His continuing espousal of values which he ascribed to feminism poses real difficulties. In part, these stem from a failure to see his relation to feminism as problematic, and from the way he views the possibility of change.

Basically, the implications of his analysis remain moral, rather than political. Rather than examine the politics of male power, he advocates a process of readjustment and educational realignment: 'The crude things in men should be educated out of them and jetisoned', he has said recently but, as Sarah Benton comments, 'It is not clear if he has any faith in this happening.'[19] Moreover, as in *The Aristos*, the vehicle for this educational process is always presented as a woman. The formula which dominates all his fiction, and much of his other comment on these issues, is that of the male pursuit of higher truths which are embodied in an elusive, existentially authentic female character offering the salvation of female values. In the novels, it is the *disappointment* of the male hero's quest which brings about any self-awareness, his very failure to contain the autonomy of the woman he pursues. In that sense, Fowles displays the disappointment and frustration of male power as a condition of male redemption. Yet in posing the issues in this form, he is also representing a realigned version of a key male myth, an idealisation which reimposes in a new form the old redemptive role which sees woman as a corrective force in relation to men.

One of Fowles's most recent critics, Peter Conradi, has commented on this 'oddly complacent kind of feminism': 'For Fowles the *ewig Weibliche* repeatedly subserves the male by modifying, civilising, forgiving and educating the stupefying power of masculine brutality and egoism, and women tend to appear in his romances as tutors, muses, sirens, nannies and gnomic trustees of the mysteriousness of existence.'[20] This aspect of Fowles's thinking is apparent throughout his writing. It marks the contradiction between a progressive recognition that men must change, and a nostalgic desire that women should do the job for them. In his 'Notes on an Unfinished Novel' he writes, 'My female characters tend to dominate the male. I see man as a kind of artifice, and woman as a kind of reality. The one is cold idea, the other is warm fact. Dædalus faces Venus, and Venus must win.'[21] In a 1974 interview, James Campbell asked him 'In all of your novels and in the longest stories in *The Ebony Tower*, the female characters have had the edge on the men in terms of awareness and knowledge of themselves. Do you believe in some sort of female principle?' Fowles answered

> Yes. I feel that the universe is female in some deep way. I think one of the things that is lacking in our society is equality of male and female ways of looking at life. I've always disliked the dominant theme of machismo as in Hemingway and the whole of American society. This sort of thing in one's writing really doesn't come out in one's conscious mind: it comes out in how one was born, the culture one was brought up in. Which is what I was trying to say in *The Collector*.

Campbell went on to ask whether Fowles was conscious that 'in all your novels the men have been, so to speak, blind at first and have come to greater awareness of their real selves in the arms of the women?' Fowles replied 'Yes, especially in *The French Lieutenant's Woman*. This is the sort of existential thesis of the books—that one has to discover one's feelings.'[22]

For Fowles, then, the female is seen in relation to the male. Women epitomise redemptive values which combine existential authenticity with a more 'natural' way of looking at life, which links with Fowles's own inclinations towards ecology and Zen Buddhism.[23] There are two connected problems in this formulation, and they demonstrate the contemporary significance of Fowles's case: one is the idealising mystification of women in itself and its relation to a male view of feminism; the other is the latent male erotic lying behind the quest for the ideal woman.

In the view of feminist novelist and critic Angela Carter, 'All the mythic versions of women, from the myth of the redeeming purity of the virgin to that of the healing, reconciling mother, are consolatory nonsenses', but they are nonsenses whose function is to promote and augment male power.[24] During and since the Victorian era, the male mythologising of women as a resolution for male doubt has taken specific forms which have been realigned to suit the imperatives of changing circumstances. Victorian men of the middle class tended to spiritualise their women as worshipful saints, to fill an empty heaven with domestic angels. Leslie Stephen apologised to his wife that 'I have not got any saints and you must not be angry if I put you in the place where my saints ought to be.'[25] Stephen epitomises a crisis of belief within a certain group of men in the late nineteenth century, a crisis which partially resolved itself in the form of a religion of personal relationships whose terms of reference were based on male prerogatives.

The contradictions involved for the contemporary male can be measured by some of Fowles's more recent views, in which his affiliation with feminism comes into conflict with his awareness of the more radical versions it has taken. In a conversation with Raman Singh published in 1980, Fowles remarks 'I'm totally for the feminine principle, as I hope all my novels prove', and he defined the feminine principle in 'a Jungian sense, I suppose. I would say I have a feminine mind.' His further comments are revealing:

> I think the female principle links women, while the male one separates men. There are certain aspects of women's liberation that seem to me rather silly. It always worries me when I see the female principle itself being attacked by women. I think there are aspects, for example, the aggressive advocation of lesbianism, that seem to me to deny it. It's not that it's worse than the gay world, but it's simply that this is denying the extraordinary half-maternal, half-mysterious aspect of women. I think they're very foolish to destroy all that.
>
> I feel a great sympathy for them. They've had such a lousy deal for the last three thousand years.[26]

Fowles's unease about radical feminism resurfaced in Sarah Benton's interview with him in 1983, and his comments to her display a devious recuperation of women back within the frame of the male imagination which contradicts his assent to feminism. When Sarah Benton remarked that Fowles's female characters are always beautiful, his response was 'I'm very naughty about that.'[27] She reports him as being 'defensively apologetic' about his divergence from feminism over the question of sexuality and 'eroticism': 'Is it very wicked to say this? We shouldn't suppress the mysterious quality in eroticism. It denies all pleasure in life.' He has short shrift for feminists who suggest that all sexual relationships with men are expressions of sadism and masochism: 'That is a perverted way of looking at sexual relationships. There are countless cases, from violence to awful rape, which you must look at in terms of sadism; but there's an overwhelming number where love is the most enriching human experience. If you start talking like this, you are saying there is something fundamentally evil in people, because there is always this root of cruelty.' Sarah Benton asked Fowles whether the two distinct characteristics which feminists of the last decade had identified in their relationship to maleness—which she sees as the fear of male violence and a profound bodily alienation—should be absent from his work; in other words, should he censor such sexism in himself. His reply was 'It surpasses the powers of man's imagination... It's a fault in my masculine thinking. I still find the women I know very well psychologically puzzling. They are still enigmatic especially when they appear to me irrational.'[28]

The unacceptability of radical feminism to Fowles, and his own admissions here, indicate the extent to which his analysis of masculinity remains caught within the limits of the male myths he seeks to confront. He displays the unease and insecurity of the contemporary male for whom the insights of liberation offered by feminism also threaten his power and status. No doubt sincere in themselves, his views of feminism are necessarily suspect and overtly contradictory by virtue of the very fact that they come from a male position. Claims as to the values and goals of feminism have a quite different function and meaning when women make them on their own behalf than they do when men make them. When women assert values as 'feminist' or 'female', even those which have been traditionally ascribed to them within patriarchal ideology, their activity declares a conception of themselves as part of a process of self-definition. When a man adopts the same arguments, their political function changes quite simply because of the relationship between those arguments, whose aim is to challenge male power, and male power itself. One must inevitably suspect a conscious or unconscious attempt to contain their impact, or somehow subvert or appropriate the cutting edge of feminism by containing it within male-defined limits. The progressive male's affiliation with feminism remains contradictory if only because it can have the effect of appropriating the spaces which women have so arduously carved out for themselves. More pertinently, a man cannot call himself 'feminist' in any real political sense because the continuing reality of male power, from which the individual man cannot simply abdicate however sympathetic to feminism he is, prevents any such simple alignment, or at the very least throws it into sharp contradiction.

This paradox forms the dialectic of Fowles's fictions. While all his male characters are men in crisis, analysed as case-studies of contemporary masculinity, they are also the temporary consumers of the imaginary women who offer them the salvation of the female; and behind the male character lurks the voyeuristic male writer-reader. What provides the dynamic for this imaginative appropriation is the hunt structure which underlies the design of the novels.

In his book *The Secular Scripture*, Northrop Frye has suggested that 'the hunt is normally an image of the masculine erotic, a movement of pursuit and linear thrust, in which there are sexual overtones to the object being hunted.'[29] Fowles's views agree with this. 'I find it difficult to think fictionally except in terms of quest, solitude, sexuality, the mania for freedom', he has said:[30] 'Sexual relations have always interested me, and problems of freedom, problems of search and quest, and I think the nucleus of all that was definitely in this whole Celtic thing from the tenth century onwards.'[31] The reference to the 'Celtic thing' indicates one correlative for his obsession, the traditions of courtly love whose literature Fowles read 'omnivorously' at Oxford (*ET*, p.119) and which itself has something to say about masculinity in that particular social formation. Behind what Fowles has called the 'mania for chivalry, courtly love, mystic and crusading Christianity, the Camelot syndrome' (*ET*, p.120) lie, as the American critic Robert Huffaker puts it, several even stranger monsters, not the least of which was the conflict between chivalry's female-orientated tradition of courtly love and its male-dominated compulsion to adventure and violence. Centuries of males have flown to war and arms while protesting that they could not love their women so much, loved they not honour more. Masculine power politics still threatens modern mankind. It is no wonder that Fowles, in his 'Personal Note', calls the Watergate tragedy more cultural than political.[32]

In the romance tradition, what Fowles describes as the 'frustrated longing and sexual irresolution, stemming out of courtly love'[33] forms a contradictory amalgam of idealisms, sexual questing and violence. For Fowles, the courtly love phenomenon expressed 'a desperately needed attempt to bring more civilisation (more female intelligence) into a brutal society' (*ET*, p.124), and perhaps this is what his own versions of the male quest imply in their neo-existential equation of search, sexuality and freedom. But by posing the existential quest for true being in terms of the quest for an ideal woman, Fowles creates a double bind: whilst showing his male characters as needing educating out of their maleness, the very design of the narrative reproduces the male fantasy of woman as the repository of higher truth. It is part of the form which his own masculine ideology takes that the novels idealise women as the bearers of true values and at the same time allow him to exercise imaginative power over them.

In part, what is in question here is the role of fiction itself and the problems of analysing masculinity in fictional terms. Inevitably, it raises the issue of sexual fantasy. There are two interrelated aspects to this, one involving the writer himself and his view of fiction, the other involving the relation between the text and the male reader. In terms of the first, Fowles's psychoanalytic understanding of fiction and fantasy indicates the ideological limits to his conception of novel writing. In terms of the second, the ideological position of the male reader needs to be brought into relation with this and questioned. For the sake of clarity, we can deal with these two points in turn, but their interaction is perhaps what should be borne in mind.

The fantasy potential of fiction depends on a relation between author, text and reader in which gender can be a crucial factor. Emmanuel Reynaud, in his recent essay on the social construction of masculinity, puts it this way: 'Art offers some men the opportunity of moulding their feminine archetypes while providing other men with the necessary images to nourish their own fantasies... In art, man expresses his dreams of appropriating women as well as appropriating the women of his dreams; and he achieves both in real life relationships with women all the better for having created standards of beauty and behaviour.'[34] In other words, there is a relationship between fantasy and power. In this process, art constructs representations which, in the words of the English media analyst Stephen Heath, help 'to make up the myth of "sexuality" which is central to the current ordering of life and lives'.[35] If art is imbued with the dominant sexual ideology, the novel and fiction have a large part to play in the articulation of narratives which seem to make sense of that ideology. For Heath, 'the novel occupies what is still in some sense a privileged position, fulfils the crucial role of the work of *saying* sex and sexuality, of giving a solid mesh of meanings, of making available sense.'[36] One might argue as to the scope of the novel's influence in terms of audience but it would be difficult to deny the strong hold over people's imaginations of the narrative model established through fiction, whether in literary forms or in its transposition to other media such as television. Within that process, not only are there unspoken presuppositions to do with sexual ideology; it also involves the active promotion of images which feed and reinforce such presuppositions.

We can see this at work in Fowles's psychoanalytic understanding of his own writing, the import of which is to see writing as an act of male self-consolation, the result of the Oedipal trauma.

In his interview with Melvyn Bragg for the 'South Bank Show' in 1982, Fowles described the obsession which 'drives all of us who are novelists I think, that is the search for the lost relationship of the mother'.[37] It is an idea which he has often articulated, but most notably in his 1977 essay 'Hardy and the Hag'. Here Fowles acknowledges that his own psychoanalytic understanding of novel-writing has been shaped by an American psychiatrist, Gilbert Rose. In 1972, Rose published an essay on *The French Lieutenant's Woman* in which he analysed the 'unconscious significance' of the

20

novel to its author. The essay put forward a theory of novel-writing which Fowles has referred to on a number of occasions as being synonymous with, or even as having helped to shape, his own views.[38] Rose's theory sees artistic creation as a compensatory act of recovery of a 'lost territory [which] is the original dual unity with the mother'.[39] This recovery is a temporary 'regaining of safety', which, if prolonged, is 'psychological death' for the male, since it threatens the male ego with the seeming nullity of fusion with the female.[40] In the 'Hardy and the Hag' essay, Fowles finds this theory 'a plausible and valuable model' regardless of its empirical truth, and he acknowledges that Rose's views 'largely confirmed—and greatly clarified—intuitive conclusions of my own.'[41] What Rose's ideas did was to confirm for Fowles a definably 'male' quality in his activity as a novelist. Using Rose, he goes so far as to argue that successful novelistic creation must almost necessarily derive from men, since male children are more likely to have undergone the separation trauma, the loss of the mother, which provides the drive behind the imaginative act of recuperation to re-create that primary state of unity with the female figure. In Fowles's terms, Rose's 'proposition was that some children retain a particularly rich memory of the passage from extreme infancy, when the identity of the baby is merged with that of the mother, to the arrival of the first awareness of separate identity and the simultaneous first dawn of what will become the adult sense of reality; that is, they are deeply marked by the passage from a unified magical world to a discrete "realistic" one.'[42] This intensified recollection of identity and unity with the mother Fowles sees as specifically characteristic of the male artist; and, having articulated his theory in terms of a 'he', he points out that the pronoun is gender-specific:

> Sensitive female readers may not be too happy about the pronoun of this paragraph, but the theory helps explain why all through more recent human history men seem better adapted—or more driven—to individual artistic expression than women. Professor Rose points out that the chance of being conditioned by this primal erotic experience is (if one accepts Freudian theory) massively loaded towards the son. The novel is, of course, something of an exception to the general rule, but even there the characteristic male preoccupation with loss, non-fulfilment, non-consummation, is usually lacking in women writers.[43]

By this highly dubious generalisation, Fowles appropriates novel-writing as specifically male territory, but what he identifies is his own psychological bent for fantasising controlled nostalgia. Novel-writing he sees as an intensely 'onanistic and taboo-laden pursuit',[44] and integral to this is the construction of a narrative which caters for this propensity. It is here that his own affinities with Hardy become plain: 'I cannot think very critically of Hardy,' he explains, 'there is too strong a sense of shared trap, a shared predicament.'[45] Hardy's predicament lies in his recurring fantasy pursuit of the elusive ideal woman, the Well-Beloved, 'that eternal other woman, the mother'. Her unattainable presence is the centre of Hardy's imaginative activity as a male novelist: 'The vanished young mother of infancy is quite as elusive as the Well-Beloved', Fowles argues, 'indeed, she *is* the Well-Beloved, although the adult writer transmogrifies her according to the pleasures and fancies that have in the older man superseded the nameless ones of the child—most commonly into a young female sexual ideal of some kind, to be attained or pursued (or denied) by himself, hiding behind some male character.'[46]

It is specifically the denial of prolonged consummation that holds the greatest imaginative power for the male writer according to Fowles. The frustration extends the pleasure by inviting a future re-creation. The novel is a titillating dalliance with desire through fantasy, a 'heuristic' process perhaps,[47] but one designed to male specification. Of Hardy's fantasies Fowles writes, 'This *abnormally* close juxtaposition, or isolating, of a male and a female character is so constant a feature of the male novel that I think it adds further support to Professor Rose's theory. I know myself how excitement mounts—if there had been a Creator, how much he must have looked forward to the chapter of Eden—as such situations approach.'[48] The self-perpetuating activity of novelistic fantasy, in which the pursuit of an ideal woman forms such a part, are for Fowles the male writer's compensation for the psychological trauma of the Oedipal split; and the male novelist is an addicted voyeur, continually re-enacting fantasies designed to reappropriate the lost mother and to then deny that reunion. As he suggests, 'To a psyche like Hardy's, both highly devious and highly erotic, it is not at all axiomatic that the happy consummation is more pleasurable' since 'the doomed and illicit hunt is still far more attractive than no hunt at all'.[49]

It is into this context that Fowles introduces his own neo-existential pursuit of the female. The elusiveness of the Well-Beloved arises from her role as a surrogate for the lost mother and from her role as representing a promised redemption. She is one of 'the maternal muses who grant the power to comprehend and palliate the universal condition of mankind, which is, given the ability of the human mind to choose and imagine other than the chosen or the actual course of events, a permanent state of loss'.[50] Yet her elusive quality is also the product of the male novelist's manipulative fantasy. Fowles puts these interconnections in such a way as to leave no doubt about the fundamental point: 'this endlessly repeated luring-denying nature of [Hardy's] heroines is not too far removed from what our more vulgar age calls the cock-tease.'[51] The Well-Beloved acts as 'a prime source of fantasy and of guidance, like Ariadne with her thread',[52] the guidance and the fantasy being, we may deduce, one and the same thing.

What Fowles describes through Hardy and through Rose's theories is a view of novel-writing modelled on the circularity and insufficiency of male desire. What is notable about his formulation is the extent of his self-awareness about the function of the novel as sexual fantasy and his correspondingly uncritical articulation of it. For feminists, such a blatant exposé may simply confirm the extent to which Fowles is caught within the limits of masculine ideology. In this sense, he exemplifies the *use* of women within the contemporary male imagination and the way that, according to its requirements, that imagination demands that women act simultaneously as existential mentors and titillating sirens. From this view, his fictions are more 'consolatory nonsense', myths of power which offer both the vicarious appropriation of imaginary women figures and the correspondingly pleasurable denial—all of which would put his relation with feminism into the category of an insidious revenge. To this equation we must add the ingredient of his extensive popularity and sales. When it was suggested in an interview that he might have 'ambivalent feelings about being the writer of best-sellers', Fowles's response was tellingly honest:

Well, I suppose I partly share the assumption that anything that sells well must be rather bad, that it must be a prostitution of some kind. I mean, I know I have one gift, which is for narrative. I can tell stories and make people listen, and I sometimes think that I abuse that talent. I suppose a parallel in sex would be a skilled seducer knowing his skill. Laying women right, left and centre, just as an exercise of skill.[53]

Quite plausibly, what Fowles's fictions may offer is a not-so-surreptitious revision of male mythologies to bolster the contemporary male ego bruised by feminism and by its own sense of crisis.

Such arguments might well undermine the credibility of seeing in Fowles's work a potential critique of masculinity and male power. Personally, I don't think they do. If the blatancy of his ideas in 'Hardy and the Hag' display the limits of his thinking, they also expose a critical self-awareness, a contradictory desire to reveal male ideology at work. It is notable, for example, how explicit he is about the deviousness of the male imagination. The function of his exposés, here or in the novels, depends in part upon the reader's own position, of course: they are there to be read, an active process in which the ideology and gender of the reader help shape the 'meaning'. Thus, while a number of male critics have rather uncritically celebrated his 'feminism',[54] one of the noticeably few women who have written about Fowles, Constance Hieatt, has argued that he displays 'a parodoxical lack of sensitivity to a woman's point of view in much of his work', and that 'although he specialises in male weaklings', he can hardly be described as a writer with a 'distinctly feminist tone'.[55]

The problem indicated here is of a wider nature than simply the 'misreading' of a text, or the limits of what Jonathan Culler calls 'male readings',[56] though as we shall see there are overt examples of that in the criticism of Fowles's works. It is also a matter of the interrelation between the ideology of a male reader and the contradictory constructions of that ideology offered by Fowles's fictions. An analysis by a male critic of the ideology of a male writer is likely to suffer, consciously and unconsciously, from blind spots similar to those indicated in Fowles's own thinking, and as such should declare itself as part of the very problem it is trying to analyse.

It is a lesson which Fowles himself has gradually learnt to put into practice in his work by presenting his own activity as a male novelist as problematic. However ambiguous, it is perhaps this self-awareness that justifies seeing in his fictions the potential for a serious critique of masculinity and the male writer's analysis of his own experience. His demythologising tends to leave the contradictions exposed, rather than resolving them: as he told Melvyn Bragg, 'I like endings where the reader is left in a kind of worry and anxiety.'[57] Such sentiments suggest both an anti-authoritarian conception of the novel as a form and a correspondingly paradoxical design upon his readers, pursuading them of the potential for free choice by manipulating their responses. Fowles's stated aim is 'not teaching the reader, but helping the reader teach himself'.[58] If in part this entails exposing to men the nature of their power, the paradoxes of this project in terms of fiction are revealed by Fowles's acknowledgement that 'I teach better if I seduce.'[59] For the male reader at least, the seductiveness of Fowles's fiction offers a hall of mirrors, from which he can discern exactly 'what's wrong with that man'; but for that to happen, the mirrors and their subjects must themselves be seen as part of the problem.

2

Bluebeard and the voyeurs:
The Collector

In writing *The Collector*, Fowles touched a nerve which has become increasingly sensitive in recent discussions about men—that of male violence against women and its relation to male sexuality. Clegg with his chloroform pad represents a male syndrome which Fowles described in an interview in 1974: 'I've always been interested in the Bluebeard syndrome, and really, that book [*The Collector*] was simply embodying it in one particular case. It's really a casebook for me.'[1] Fowles has said that the idea was developed from Bartok's opera *Bluebeard's Castle*, which contains 'the symbolism of the man imprisoning women underground' and which he synthesised with a contemporary newspaper report 'of a boy who captured a girl and imprisoned her in an air-raid shelter at the end of his garden... there were many peculiar features about this case that fascinated me.'[2]

The Collector is a 'casebook' in a number of ways. It sets a pattern for the later fiction by presenting a central male character as a case-study of particular forms of masculine behaviour. Fowles's declared interest in the early case-studies of Freud as almost 'fictional' psychoanalytic narratives links with this, although the narrative approach of *The Collector* is not directly analytical.[3] Equally, Clegg is a case-study of male behaviour in general: he is symptomatic of the male idealisation of women and of the way male power both feeds on and enforces itself through such idealisation. More problematically, the novel is a casebook of Fowles's own latent contradictions about the whole subject and his declared fascination for it, since, partly by virtue of its very narrative strategies, the book invites an almost voyeuristic interest from the reader. It is a point which suggests that Fowles himself is

27

a kind of Bluebeard, parading fantasies of power whose 'appeal' is thoroughly ambiguous. To elucidate this idea, it will be as well if we look in turn at the different ways in which the book functions.

As a case-study, the central male character Clegg embodies that classic schizophrenia of the male psyche which has institutionalised itself in sexual ideology by being perversely projected onto and superimposed upon women. Clegg is both Caliban and Ferdinand, the monster and the prince (C, p.199), the two polar opposites of the male spectrum. Miranda recognises it after her attempt to 'seduce' him, what she sees as 'this weird male thing. Now I'm no longer nice. They sulk if you don't give, and hate you when you do. Intelligent men must despise themselves for being like that. Their illogicality.' (C, p.254). The classic male view of women as madonnas to be worshipped and whores to be reviled always did say more about men than it ever could about women since it is precisely patriarchal ideology which invents and imposes the categorisation. It speaks of the male fear of women, sexuality and female sexuality specifically, a fear which paradoxically comes out of and gives rise to a need to repress the mother in order to maintain male power and control.[4] One literary version of this male schizophrenia is Robert Louis Stevenson's Dr Jekyll and Mr Hyde (1886).[5] Like Shakespeare's Ferdinand/Caliban model, and Hardy's Angel Clare/Alec d'Urberville, it poses the sexual split in terms of men rather than expressing it in terms of women, as patriarchal ideology does normally. The perverse Hyde is the idealist Jekyll's alter ego. The contradictions between the rational and the sexual, between authoritarian control and irrational passion, are shown as centred within the male as the pivots of patriarchy. Like Stevenson's text, The Collector presents this schizophrenia, with its accompanying wille zür macht, in action: Clegg's Jekyll-and-Hyde responses are seen being projected onto Miranda and, by making him both Ferdinand and Caliban, the book suggests that he is the prototype of masculinity. The critical overview in the book is provided through a narrative which presents Clegg dialectically, from his own position and from Miranda's; but this 'inside story' approach has its own peculiar repercussions.

Clegg's narrative shows him to be both the perpetrator and the

victim of the paradoxes of male power. In his case they take a
specific and aggravated form, but the book allows us to see all men
as potential if not actual Cleggs—collectors, possessors,
controllers, using power to compensate for inadequacy. Fowles
has described his view of the 'narcissistic and parasitical' hobby of
collecting and its links with totalitarianism: 'Any one who still
collects (i.e. kills) some field of living life just for pleasure and
vanity has all the makings of a concentration-camp
commandant.'[6] Clegg's collector mentality is a compensation for
his sense of personal deficiency. Sexually, he is split. His desire for
'higher aspirations' (C, p.12) and his rejection of the 'crude animal
thing I was born without' (C, p.10), and which he sees in the men
at work, are the other side of the coin to his evasively expressed
fascination for pornography, sex as passive consumption. The two
are manifest in his dreams about Miranda. The 'nice dreams' are
the ones in which she enacts roles in which both of them achieve
an ideal middle-class marriage—'Nothing nasty', Clegg insists,
but 'of course the other men all green round the gills.' (C. p.6)
The other dreams occurred after seeing her out with another man:
'I let myself dream I hit her across the face as I saw it done once by
a chap in a telly play.' (C, p.7) The two sides are brought together
in his dreams about Miranda being attacked, in which Clegg is
both her rescuer and 'the man that attacked her, only I didn't hurt
her; I captured her' (C, p.16). Clegg's 'idealism' is seen to be one
and the same as his urge to possess, and this forms part of a wider
theme. Fowles's men cannot see what they are doing to other
people because of a constitutional self-centred egoism which is
central to the social legacy of masculinity, part of its 'crust'. Clegg
cannot believe that Miranda will not at some point accept and
understand him: 'if she's with me, she'll see my good points' (C,
p.17) he thinks and, worryingly, some male critics have been
inclined to agree with him. The American, Peter Wolfe, who is the
most overtly male-orientated of Fowles's critics, quotes and
seemingly endorses a comment by Thomas Churchill in which he
says of Clegg and Miranda 'The boy and girl are not really much
different... they might find a way if they worked at it hard
enough.'[7] This suggests an astounding blindness to the realities of
male violence and possession but, as we shall see in the other

novels, it is by no means untypical of the approaches some male critics adopt to Fowles's work.

Clegg's emotional and sexual fascism is common to all Fowles's male characters, though it differs in degree of intensity or overtness. The situation of locking Miranda up is, of course, both a real possibility and a metaphorical model, marriage being the most obvious analogy and one the book overtly suggests on a number of occasions (*C*, pp.51, 149). The interesting point is the way this situation is related to more general elements in male ideology and power.

Fowles has suggested that Clegg is to be seen as a product of his time, historically shaped by accelerating consumer capitalism and the seedy reality of the acquisitive society of the late 1950s. In the preface to *The Aristos*, Fowles explains the book in terms of its being a 'parable' dealing with class and inequality, the conflict between his own problematic categories, 'the Few and the Many': 'I tried to show that his evil was largely, perhaps wholly, the result of a bad education, a mean environment, being orphaned: all factors over which he has no control.' (*A*, p.10) Clegg's turning of living things into objects to be possessed can be equated with what Fowles identifies as the 'tendency of any capitalist society [which] is to turn all experiences and relationships into objects' (*A*, p.164). It is a case of Fowles showing Clegg as the product of his environment and reproducing its dominant values—capitalism, masculinity and neo-fascism forming an equation which Fowles hovers uneasily around more explicitly in the later novels.

Yet Clegg is far from being a 'macho' male. He is, even in Miranda's view, 'Exactly the sort of man you would *not* suspect. The most unwolf like.' (*C*, p.128) Part of his problem is precisely an inability to measure up to a stereotypical male image, an outcome of his upbringing if we take Fowles's views in *The Aristos* seriously. The early death of his father, and his mother who 'went off soon after' (*C*, p.7), left him with his aunt and uncle. Though Uncle Dick was 'as good as a father' (*C*, p.8), Clegg's situation is close to that which Fowles has outlined as the 'predisposing cause in outright paedophilia'—an 'unloving or rejecting mother, and a father who fails to provide the "male model" of the standard Oedipal situation. The child-victim will thus be turned in and self-fixed at an exceptionally early age.'[8] It would be inaccurate to apply this to Clegg directly, but it demonstrates Fowles's own predisposition to understand male sexual phenomena in terms of their relations to the wider social and psychological construction of masculine models. Clegg is not a 'normal' male, but only in the extent to which he acts out his fantasies of power.

In Clegg's case, the pursuit of power as a compensation for his insecurities is managed through his pools win. 'Money is Power', he asserts with a characteristic cliché: 'In my opinion a lot of people who may seem happy now would do what I did or similar things if they had the money and the time.' (C, p.23) Reading about his own abduction of Miranda in the newspapers 'gave me a feeling of power, I don't know why.' (C, p.44) He institutes their 'relationship' on a basis which he controls physically and economically, but in which he is dependent upon her emotionally: 'She always seemed to get me on the defensive. In my dreams it was always the other way round. . . In my dreams it was always we looked into each other's eyes one day and then we kissed and nothing was said until after.' (C, p.37) 'You want to lean on me', Miranda tells him, 'I expect it's your mother. You're looking for your mother.' Clegg suggests to her 'You could lean on me financially', to which she retorts 'And you on me for everything else? God forbid.' (C, p.63) What Clegg wants from Miranda is the impossible compensation for his own sense of loss and desire[9] and the only way he can get that is through forcing her into the role of embodying his fantasies. As Miranda later realises, 'I'm not acting like the girl of his dreams I was. I'm his pig in a poke.' (C, p.246)

Clegg sees himself as 'a cruel king' (C, p.41) and models his control of Miranda significantly enough on tactics gleaned from a book called *Secrets of the Gestapo* (C, p.44). Miranda's self-analogy with Anne Frank (C, p.233) confirms the neo-fascist element we are invited to see in Clegg. Equally, however, his desire for power over her finds its expression in a thoroughly romanticised idealism. He fantasises that she will become submissively doll-like and allow him to 'love' her (C, p.37). He embodies a nostalgically 'old-fashioned' attitude of being 'in love', although he knows that, according to a 'chap called Nobby in the RAPC who knew all about women. . . you shouldn't ever tell a woman you loved her.

Even if you did.' (*C*, p.37) He presents his love in terms of romantic clichés whose function is to indicate how second-hand a part of sexual ideology Clegg's views are: Miranda becomes 'the purpose of my life' (*C*, p.20); 'I knew my love was worthy of her' (*C*, p.30); 'you're all I've got that makes life worth living' (*C*, p.54); 'It was like we were the only two people in the world' (*C*, p.68). But at the same time these clichés are self-exposing, they also serve to probe the ideology of romantic love itself, to reveal how analogous it is to Clegg's possessiveness. Like William Blake's 'The Clod and the Pebble', Clegg's case suggests that the selfless idealism of love is merely the inverse of its possessive impulse; under patriarchal forms, love relationships are predicated as power battles serving male interests.

Romantic idealism and a desire for power, then, are in Clegg's terms the same, since both turn women into instruments for male gratification. The connection becomes clear in his obsessive need to take photographs of Miranda. The American feminist Andrea Dworkin has argued that the pornographic photograph is 'the ultimate tribute to male power: the male is not in the room, yet the women are there for his pleasure. His wealth produces the photograph; his wealth consumes the photograph; he produces and consumes women.'[10] Clegg's interest is in the passive image of Miranda, an object which is his imagined version of her rather than her as a person. It is a form of self-desire enacted through the use of another and, according to the novelist André Malraux, a feature of male desire itself.[11]

When Miranda demonstrates that she *is* autonomous and challenges his fantasies, he reacts with force, to make her passive and turn her back into a controllable image. Thus, when she attempts to escape, having realised that he will not keep his promise to let her go, it is then that he re-uses the chloroform pad, strips her whilst she is unconscious and photographs her: 'It was like I'd showed who was really the master.' (*C*. p.94) Even more decisive is the episode shortly after when Miranda tries to break Clegg's hold over her by giving herself to him sexually. As this is her initiative, the fact of Clegg's impotence is all the more agonising to him: 'She made me look a proper fool... I felt she was despising me, I was a freak.' (*C*, p.110) It is this that shatters

Clegg's illusions but he blames her sexual overtness for his reactions: she 'killed all the romance, she had made herself like any other woman' (*C*, p.114). As a result he feels quite justified in asking her to pose for more photographs—'You took your clothes off, you asked for it. Now you got it.' (*C*, p.118) What he finally hates about Miranda is precisely that she *is* real and that she does not subserve his idea of her, and because of that she exposes rather than allays his insecurities. His reaction is to twist his idealism inside out, showing its real basis in a desire for power as he humiliates and degrades her. His consolation now is the photographs which 'prove' his sexual capacity:

> Because I could do it.
> The photographs (the day I gave her the pad),
> I used to look at them sometimes. I could take my time with them. They
> didn't talk back at me.
> (*C*, p.113)

Miranda's response is 'Oh, God you're not a man, if only you were a man' (*C*, p.121), instead of 'a dirty little masturbating worm.' (*C*, p.120)

Clegg's narrative has the same perversely psychotic quality as Browning's portrait of an equally possessive and destructive male 'lover' in 'Porphyria's Lover'. But the point is not that Clegg is abnormal. As he says disturbingly to Miranda, 'you think I'm not normal keeping you here like this. Perhaps I'm not. But I can tell you there'd be a blooming lot more of this if more people had the money and the time to do it. Anyway there's more of it now than anyone knows.' (*C*, p.75) The implication is that all men are in one sense or another complicit in a system of power relations rooted in forms of appropriation and violence as means of dominance and control. The pervasive male ways of seeing women are an appropriation, as are the patriarchal forms of the social structure which limit and confine women to certain roles, economic expectations and restricted opportunities. Their *raison d'être* is the perpetuation of male privilege in different manifestations. In sexual terms, Clegg exemplifies the forms masculinity takes in the contemporary world. All men may not act out the fantasies Clegg has in the manner in which he does, just as all men may not be actual rapists; but potentially they can and are because of the relation of social power and dominance they maintain over women. The violent forms into which sexual relations have been shaped, whether it be rape, pornography, prostitution, marital coercion, actual physical violence, psychological pressure, or whatever, are all constructed to embody and enforce dominantly male prerogatives. Fowles explores the implications of these issues through Miranda's narrative and her views of Clegg.

In a moment of perhaps unintentional directness, Miranda writes in her diary 'The ordinary man is the curse of civilisation.' (*C*, p.137) In the context, she means in the sense of class, but the statement has the obvious gender application too. That this is not fanciful becomes apparent when we discover that she associates rationalism with being male, 'all that clumsy masculine analysis' (*C*, p.140). Collecting is also male, as we might expect. Collectors, like scientists, are destructive in Miranda's eyes, 'anti-life' (*C*, p.132). They are interested in the thing as object with themselves as the dominant subject, rather than in the living relation between things of equal autonomous being. Clegg embodies this rationalistic, possessive male principle, whereas Miranda herself embodies in part a Zen-like intuition of essences and interrelatedness. By implication, this is the antidote to Clegg's self-centred male egoism. Given Fowles's own predisposition, this suggests a privileging of Miranda's narrative, but the book does not fully endorse it. She is, as Fowles himself has pointed out, 'arrogant in her ideas, a prig, a liberal-humanist snob' (*A*, p.10). While many of the values and ideas Miranda expresses are used critically to analyse Clegg, the book's strategy is to intertwine this evaluation with Miranda's reflections on her friend and mentor George Paston in such a way as to broaden the impact of the analysis to include directly other men. Unwittingly, Miranda provides in G.P. a mirror image for Clegg, another man whom she admires but who the reader can see as a version of Clegg, another *man*.

When Miranda recounts taking her friends Piers and Antoinette to meet G.P., she describes how he drove them out of his house in anger. As Miranda turned to go back, Antoinette warned 'Darling, he'll murder you' (*C*, p.179). Miranda excuses G.P.'s manners at the end of this entry in her diary because basically 'he was *sweet*'. But the very next entry opens 'I don't trust him. He's bought this house.' (*C*, p.180) The carry-over of the male pronouns links up Clegg and G.P. into interchangeable male personae. In G.P.'s case, his masculine outlook takes a more subtly invidious form. G.P. is distinguished for Miranda because 'he has (except over women) principles' (*C*, p.183). Woman are his 'one horrid weakness' (*C*, p.151). For G.P. himself, woman are 'a disease' whose name he won't reveal to Miranda since 'you don't tell diseases their names' (*C*, p.187). His brutal criticism about her own work—'It was as if he had turned and hit me with his fist... It hurt like a series of slaps across the face' (*C*, p.168)—might be excused on the grounds of artistic integrity, though his comments hardly strike the chord of being disinterested: 'you don't really stand a dog's chance anyhow. You're too pretty. The art of love's your line: not the love of art.' (*C*, p.170) What is revealed through Miranda, despite her own eventual espousal of G.P.'s philosophies of 'natural' sexuality, is his Don Juanism: he is a seducer and in that sense a collector. Like Urfe in *The Magus*, G.P.'s approach to women is to get them to feel sorry for him and then exploit them emotionally. Again, as with Urfe, the spurious decency of his recognition of this is part of the game. He slept with Miranda's friend Antoinette deliberately to 'exorcize' Miranda (*C*, p.227), and she documents his response to her own sense of injury:

He said, men are vile.
I said, the vilest thing about them is that they can say that with a smile on their faces. (*C*, p.190).

In his attitude to Miranda, G.P. is also shown as fantasising his relations with women into romantic illusions of being 'in love'. When Miranda tells Clegg the beauty and the beast story, she says 'now it's your turn to tell a fairy story'. Clegg replies 'I love you' and Miranda's comment on his words is 'They were quite hopeless. He said it as he might have said, I have cancer.' (*C*, p.199-200) G.P.'s view of being 'in love' is that it is a constitutional hazard for men: 'You've never been deeply in love. Perhaps you

35

never will be. He said, love goes on happening to you. To men.'
(C, p.226) Clegg's reaction to his 'love' for Miranda is to capture
her and lock her up. G.P.'s is to send her away, to stop seeing her
because 'I can't go on being disturbed by you.' (C, p.226) Both
reactions are equally self-centred in outlook, and both men
exercise their power over her. The suspicion even crosses
Miranda's mind that G.P.'s decision to send her away was a
gambit of sexual politics in order to catch her, 'a trap. Like a
sacrifice in chess. Supposing I had said on the stairs, do what you
like with me, but don't send me away?' (C, p.230) This echoes her
comment to Clegg after their walk round the garden, when she felt
he wanted to kiss her: she makes him promise not to do anything to
her 'in a mean way. I mean don't knock me unconscious or
chloroform me again or anything. I shan't struggle, I'll let you do
what you like.' (C, p.67) At times her view of G.P. could be
directly interchangeable with her speculations about Clegg in the
shared ambivalence of their motives and behaviour: 'Of course
G.P. was always trying to get me into bed. I don't know why but I
see that more clearly now than I ever did at the time. He shocked
me, bullied me, taunted me—never in nasty ways. Obliquely. He
didn't even force me in any way. Touch me. I mean, he respected
me in a queer way.' (C, p.192) Her relations with both men have
the nature of a battle or power struggle in which she is the
subjected victim.

In both cases, the romantic illusions are seen as an aspect of the
male urge to control. This is confirmed at the point when
Miranda recognises Clegg's own Jekyll-and-Hyde personality,
which we see as synonymous with the other two men in the book.
Of Clegg she writes, 'Deep down in him, side by side with the
beastliness, the sourness, there is a tremendous innocence. It rules
him. He must protect it.' (C, p.252) It is an insecurity about
feelings, particularly sexual, which leads to a defensive imposition
of power and a desire to possess. This 'weird male thing' is Clegg's
'secret' (C, p.254), a sexual and emotional impotence: 'He can't do
it. There's no man in him.' (C, p.252) Later Miranda is suddenly
convinced of 'The power of women! I've never felt so full of
mysterious power. Men are a joke.' (C, p.258) The joke is partly
the contradiction between feeling and fear, the need for and fear of

dependency unless under the male prerogative. The other man in Miranda's life, Piers, exhibits the same syndrome. When, in France, Miranda met Jean-Louis, Piers reaction was 'crude... That stupid clumsy frightened-of-being-soft English male cruelty to the truth... that arrogance, that insensitivity of boys who've been to public schools.' (*C*, p.210-11) G.P. demonstrates a similar split. When Miranda daydreams about him she recognises her illusions for what they are:

> I've been daydreaming (not for the first time) about living with G.P. He deceives me, he leaves me, he is brutal and cynical with me, I am in despair. In these daydreams there isn't much sex, it's just our living together. In rather romantic surroundings... We are together, very close in spirit. All silly magazine stuff, really, in the details. But there is the closeness of spirit. That is something real. And the situations I imagine (where he forsakes me) are real. I mean, it kills me to think of them. (*C*, p.245)

The intriguing point here is not simply that this shows Miranda doing to G.P. what Clegg and G.P. do to her—making him up and fantasising about him, though crucially on totally different terms and with an awareness of the nature of her fantasies. It also demonstrates the narrative's own self-consciousness about the central issues of enacting ideological roles, pre-existent sexual models, the social fictions and scripts of gender.

So far, we have looked at the book and the characters as evidence of a case-study of masculinity, but to take this as unproblematic is to run the risk of falling into the contradictions within the book itself. Clegg is not, after all, a 'real' person whom we can simply take as providing insights into male behaviour. Fowles has said that he 'tried to write in terms of the strictest realism' in the book[12] and this is apparent; but necessarily we need to remain aware that the book is a fictional construction within Fowles's jurisdiction as a male author. Characteristically, Fowles makes use of this awareness of fictionality in order to explore how men impose and act out roles, but we also see the book's narrative working in ways which need investigating and exposing for their own latent sexual politics and Fowles's male assumptions.

As an initial point, it is noticeable that the book uses other 'fictions' as a ground for its narrative situation, most obviously *The*

Tempest and, to a lesser extent, Jane Austen's *Emma*. This tactic calls attention to the playing-out of roles, which are themselves fantasies, as they are transposed from the past onto the present. This helps to lay bare the way in which the male characters in particular are subject to a social mythology of masculinity, acting parts in the existing script of sexuality as it is presented in social ideology. 'Caliban is Mr Elton. Piers is Frank Churchill. But is G.P. Mr Knightley?' Miranda asks, exasperated at 'the awful problem of *the* man.' (*C*, p.230) This strategy of calling attention to fictional roles as a way of exposing the social myths of masculinity and gender is one of the central elements of Fowles's analysis in his fiction, and *The Collector* establishes it as a continuing means of investigation. It also makes a dialectical point about masculinity as social ideology. In the roles they play out and force on women, men have the power, a political reality which cannot be forgotten without losing the central issue. But within these roles, men themselves remain bound and constricted by the masculine crust, by the very limits of masculinity, to use Tolson's phrase. In a very real sense, then, Miranda tells Clegg 'You're the one imprisoned in a cellar' (*C*, p.62), a confinement which is forced on both him and her by the terms of power on which their 'relationship' is predicated.

Beyond Fowles's use of self-conscious fictionality, however, there remains his own masculine position from which he cannot escape as a male writer despite his self-critical awareness. This gender bias is present in the book without our needing to ascribe any of its content directly to Fowles: it is there in the way the book is structured and built.

We can illustrate this by considering the way the two narratives, Clegg's and Miranda's, function. There is an obvious dialectical effect in their interaction. By virtue of what Conradi describes as 'the gaps and disjunctures between Clegg's and Miranda's narratives',[13] the attempt at an almost common-sense coherence in Clegg's account is fractured and critically exposed, a tactic Fowles uses again in *Daniel Martin*. We realise also from the interaction between the two versions of events that, not only do they misread each other—not only is there none of the understanding Clegg expects, for example—but when Miranda does actually sympathise with him, he cannot see it. The situation makes it impossible for either to see the other as 'real': Clegg's voice enters Miranda's narrative only as 'C.' or 'Caliban', while she exists in his in inverted commas and the past tense. But we need also to ask about the function of these narratives in relation to Fowles's own imagining of the situation and his construction of them. Like Ian McEwan, he has imagined himself into circumstances which are distinctly perverse; and in terms of the way the narratives might be read, this is both an exorcism and a fascination.

The American critic Barry Olshen learned in an interview with Fowles in 1977 that the idea of framing Miranda's narrative within Clegg's was 'an afterthought and came as a recommendation from Fowles's editor. The author had originally submitted the two accounts in sequence.'[14] He goes on to make an intriguing point about the form of Miranda's narrative:

> Because of the conventional assumption in the diary form that the writer is the only reader (or, as Miranda says, that she is 'talking to herself'), we must assume that we are getting a very private glimpse into the innermost thoughts and feelings of the diarist. We are thus ironically required to imagine ourselves in an analogous role to Clegg's, the role of the voyeur, reading what was never intended for us to read, and gaining vicarious enjoyment from this experience.[15]

Whether we get 'vicarious enjoyment' or not depends on *how* the book is read and by whom. One imagines it to be a quite different reading experience for a woman than it is for a man, partly because for the male reader it must be said that the book unlocks a male fantasy which has had general currency at least since de Sade, even whilst exposing its fundamental roots in a desire for power over women. In other words, *The Collector* constructs that fantasy in self-conscious form, but ambiguously.

Fowles admitted as much in a comment in the 'Hardy and the Hag' essay. Elaborating on the '*abnormally* close juxtaposition, or isolating, of a male and a female character [which] is so constant a feature of the male novel', what he calls the 'tryst', he goes on to say this:

Though I gained the outward theme of *The Collector* from a bizarre real-life incident in the 1950s, similar fantasies had haunted my adolescence—not, let me quickly say, with the cruelties and criminalities of the book, but very much more along the lines of the Hardy tryst. That is, I dreamed isolating situations with girls reality did not permit me isolation with: the desert island, the aircrash with two survivors, the stopped lift, the rescue from a fate worse than death... all the desperate remedies of the romantic novelette; but also, more valuably, countless variations of the chance meeting in more realistic contexts. A common feature of such fantasies was some kind of close confinement, like Hardy's lerret, where the Well-Beloved was obliged to notice me; and I realise, in retrospect, that my own book was a working-out of the futility, in reality, of expecting well of such metaphors for the irrecoverable relationship. I had the very greatest difficulty in killing off my own heroine; and I have only quite recently, in a manner I trust readers will now guess, understood the real meaning of my ending... the way in which the monstrous and pitiable Clegg (the man who acts out his own fantasies) prepares for a new 'guest' in the Bluebeard's cell beneath his lonely house. It is a very grave fallacy that novelists understand the personal application of their own novels.[16]

This demonstrates Fowles's awareness of the pervasive hold over men of their mythologies of sexual power and the danger or 'futility... of expecting well of such metaphors' in reality. But it also reveals a notion of the novelist as a kind of Clegg, a collector of imagined women pursuing his own obsessions and, in the process, making available fantasies for reading. For Fowles it is both an exercising and an exorcism of power: it is after all he who 'kills' Miranda to make way for another version of the fantasy woman in another novel. But what is the relation of this to its possible readers? When Clegg is being shown round the cellar, the estate agent comments 'Just the thing for orgies' (*C*, p.19), no doubt with a knowing male wink. Is the Bluebeard syndrome simply exposed in the book, or is it at the same time obliquely catered for by the reader's illicit access to Miranda's diary and Clegg's reminiscences? Such access makes the point to the male reader at least that we are complicit voyeurs, but at the same time Miranda herself has been conceived from a male angle: 'The power of women! I've never felt so full of mysterious power... We're so weak physically, so helpless with things. Still, even today. But we're stronger than they [men] are. We can stand their cruelty. They can't stand ours.' (*C*, p.258) Is this a woman's view of this imaginary woman's experience, or a man's? And by enclosing Miranda's narrative within Clegg's, in a certain sense the book contains her within his ongoing power, mounted like a specimen for our appraisal and gaze.

This is not to suggest that Fowles was deliberately offering a perverse voyeurism for the male reader of *The Collector*, though in effect that may well be one possible reading of the book. He himself didn't expect it to be a success, according to interviewer Richard Boston, who comments, 'which of course it was'.[17] Perhaps this was modesty on the part of a newly launched novelist, but in retrospect it seems surprising and even naïve. The media popularity of *The Collector*, both in book form and as a film which Fowles himself dislikes, is a significant phenomenon. Inescapably, this is the result as much of a vicarious fascination with the lurid and perverse elements in the book as of a wish to understand or exorcise from the mind the fantasy of the male abductor-rapist with power over women. The book is notable for a certain self-awareness over this issue. When Clegg picks up copies of the papers to read about Miranda's abduction, he reveals both the function of the media in constructing and representing narratives of sexuality and, inadvertently, comments on the fantasising function of the book itself. He buys 'the tripe papers' (*C*, p.42) which carry big photographs of Miranda with headlines like '*Have You Seen This Girl?*' Clegg comments: 'They all said she was pretty. There were photos. If she was ugly it would all have been two lines on the back page. I sat in the van on the road verge on the way back and read all the papers said. It gave me a feeling of power, I don't know why.' (*C*, p.43-4) How would it have affected the reading of *The Collector* if Fowles had made Miranda 'ugly'?

Then there is Clegg's narrative itself: a confessional? To a psychiatrist, a priest, a prison warder? Certainly an address to the reader on personal terms as all the conversational asides by 'yours truly' indicate. Or, for all the forced formalities, awkwardness and evasiveness, is it a perverse kind of lover's confession? In *The History of Sexuality*, French theorist Michel Foucault has pointed out how the confession is symptomatic of the modern organisation of sexuality as verbal discourse, particularly of supposedly unnatural or aberrant forms of sexuality. The function of the confession is that 'it exonerates, redeems, and purifies him; it unburdens him of his wrongs, liberates him, and promises him salvation'. Foucault continues:

> Its veracity is not guaranteed by the lofty authority of the magistery, not by the tradition it transmits, but by the bonds, the basic intimacy in discourse between the one who speaks and what he is speaking about. On the other hand, the agency of domination does not reside in the one who speaks (for it is he who is constrained), but in the one who listens and says nothing; not in the one who knows and answers, but in the one who questions and is not supposed to know... It is no longer a question simply of saying what was done—the sexual act—and how it was done; but of reconstructing, in and around the act, the thoughts that recapitulated it, the obsessions that accompanied it, the images, desires, modulations, and quality of the pleasure that animated it. For the first time no doubt, a society has taken upon itself to solicit and hear the imparting of individual pleasures.[18]

There is no doubt that for Clegg his experience with Miranda was a 'pleasure', for he says as much on a number of occasions (*C*, p.282 for example). And, we remember, he is 'confessing' his pleasure after the fact, recapitulating his obsessions to, and for, the reader in preparation for a new experience. By 'listening' to Clegg's insidious confession does the reader in some peculiar way lend credence or give a certain kind of validity to his further exploits? Do we come out of the book realising that he is going to do it again and what the real implications of that are in the world outside the book? Or has it, for the male reader, provided a spurious pleasure of its own?

Probably both, a fact which, if true, expresses the male readers' own contradictory relation to the experience of masculinity. At the end of the book, Clegg's version of the male schizophrenia re-emerges. He envisages an idealised romantic fantasy as the finale for his relationship with Miranda, a farcically inappropriate Romeo and Juliet death scene in which, bereft by her death, he commits suicide alongside her. The fracture between this and his actual actions when the dead Miranda becomes literally a thing for him to dispose of epitomises the split in his psychology, the male contradiction which underpins the patriarchal control of women. Clegg's self-centred fantasy breeds Miranda's death,

Miranda says 'I could never cure him. Because I'm his disease' (*C*, p.257), but the book makes plain that what he suffers from and she dies from is his own power. Her comment suggests that men who look to women for salvation merely succeed in enmeshing them in their own webs. It is a conundrum which Fowles's next-published novel confronts in the most ambiguous terms.

of guilt, or even anger, about male social power.

If Nicholas is less overtly perverse than Clegg as an example of male attitudes, he is no less a case study of the limits of masculinity. In the museum towards the end of the original version of the book,[1] Mrs de Seitas says to him 'If there was a Department of Young Men I should certainly take you to it. I would like to have you identified.' (*M*, p.540) The label would probably be *male—predatory*. As he looks back on his experiences prior to going to Greece, the picture Urfe paints of himself is of the classic 'lone wolf'. This is specifically true of his approach to relationships, which he saw according to the needs of his own ego and which he manipulated by virtue of his social power as a male. He informs us that with women his '"technique" was to make a show of unpredictability, cynicism, and indifference. Then, like a conjurer with his white rabbit, I produced the solitary heart.' (*M*, pp.15-6) This emotional trickery was self-confessedly a 'show', a playing-out of roles rather than an attempt at real relationships. He almost literally scripted his affairs: 'I became as neat at ending liaisons as at starting them.' (*M*, p.16) His hero was D.H. Lawrence, 'the greatest human being of the century' (*M*, p.11), whose attraction for him, we learn later, lay partly in his vision of sexual relations as male dominated, 'the woman inferior to man in everything but that one great power of female dark mystery and beauty; the brilliant, virile male and the dark, swooning female.' (*M*, p.214) This male mystification led Urfe into a familiar round of the pursuit, conquest and abandonment of the different women he chanced upon: 'I didn't collect conquests; but by the time I left Oxford I was a dozen girls away from virginity. I found my sexual success and the apparently ephemeral nature of love equally pleasing. It was like being good at golf, but despising the game. One was covered all round, both when one played and when one didn't.' (*M*, p.16) Unlike Clegg, Urfe's 'disease' was, as he later identifies it, 'congenital promiscuity' (*M*, p.235), but they share the same sexual obsession with power. Alison, clearly his mentor from the beginning, 'didn't fall for the solitary heart; she had a nose for emotional blackmail' (*M*, p.28). She describes him as 'the *affaire de peau* type' (*M*, p.23). And later, during 'a white-hot outpouring of contempt for men' once Urfe has decided to leave for Greece, she calls him 'a snob, a prig, a twopenny-halfpenny Don Juan' (*M*, p.34).

The picture we get of Urfe is hardly auspicious, and the epigram from de Sade—'a professional rake is rarely a man to be pitied' (*M*, p.9)—can be read as both ironic and literal. The book's scheme is to bring Urfe to account for his exploitative attitudes by means of the masque and trial. He is, however, such an unsympathetic character even by his own report that one is tempted to question whether it is worth the effort. As he himself admits in the revised version, 'All right. I treated Alison very badly. I'm a born cad, a swine, whatever you want. But why the colossal performance just to tell one miserable moral bankrupt what he is?' (*MRV*, p.626) In Olshen's view, this casts a partial doubt over the success of the novel itself: 'Surely the main deficiency in the characterisation of Nicholas lies in his attraction for the females of the novel when he seems to have none whatsoever for the reader.'[2] It is one of the contradictions of the book that Urfe as a character does not justify the amount of time and attention spent on him. Despite Fowles's view that there is 'certainly meant to be some progression in Nicholas's character',[3] at the end of both versions he remains fundamentally unchanged in terms of his attitudes to women and his exploitation of his own social power. What change there might be we must imagine as subsequent to the events of the book, as the retrospective narrative invites us to do. And much of the time what we see of him is not simply an archetypal male but a stereotype. So why has Fowles constructed such an elaborate book around him?

There are a number of possible answers to such a question, the sheer entertainment value of the book's bewildering existential quality being one. But as far as our argument is concerned, seeing *The Magus* as an investigation of male mythologies inevitably leads into contradictions, both in the character and in Fowles's shaping of the book. It will be of use initially to look at the ways in which the character embodies central aspects of masculinity as Fowles views it and how those are investigated, before considering Fowles's own position.

It is the very typicality of Nicholas and his behaviour that is the pivot of the book's analysis. As a middle-class man of his generation, he is a walking cliché and Fowles shows him up as such. The retrospective narrative viewpoint is one way in which this is managed. Urfe is supposedly looking back over his past behaviour from the unspecified vantage point of many years (*M*, p.55). This allows not simply for detachment but for overt self-indictment giving the impression that the later Urfe can now see through his earlier manipulative attitude. Having disposed of Janet, 'a fundamentally silly girl I knew I didn't love' (*M*, p.16), he tells us he became involved with Alison in a way which struck a deeper note than his previous affairs: 'I suddenly had a feeling that we were one body, one person... A terrible deathlike feeling, which anyone less cerebral and self-absorbed than I was then would have realized was simply love. I thought it was desire. I drove her straight home and tore her clothes off.' (*M*, p.29) The later Urfe exposes how he used Alison as a stopgap before his departure for Greece. He lied about the extent of his interest in her (*M*, p.25) and was 'deceiving her with another woman during the latter part of September. The woman was Greece.' (*M*, p.33) The stagey rhetoric of his note when he left—'Oh God, if only I was worth waiting for'—is blatantly denied by the sense of relief he admits to having felt: 'The thing I felt most clearly, when the first corner was turned, was that I had escaped. Obscurer, but no less strong, was the feeling that she loved me more than I loved her, and that consequently I had in some indefinable way won.' His sense of exhileration at 'the voyage into the unknown, the taking wing again' is accompanied by 'an agreeable feeling of emotional triumph. A dry feeling; but I liked things dry.' As he walked off to Victoria station, leaving a potentially suicidal Alison behind, he recalls that he began to sing: 'it was not a brave attempt to hide my grief, but a revoltingly unclouded desire to sing.' (*M*, p.41)

This note of self-criticism takes us into a sympathy with the narrating voice which it would be impossible to give his former self and it exposes the clichés he previously acted out. Here we have Urfe as a 1950s version of Clint Eastwood, what Fowles has described as 'the idiotic and ithyphallic James Bond'[4] image—cool, in control, untouched by feeling or involvement, using his relationships and the power of his privileged status to bolster his own ego. The note of Chandler-like parody in 'a dry feeling; but I liked things dry' is there as a tactic to show Urfe acting out the self-delusions of male imagery. The strategy of self-exposure is a continuing one throughout the book. It maintains the suggestion of a potential for change but it is a notion which, as we shall see, the book structurally discourages us from seeing as a real possibility except outside of this fiction. And equally, it also functions as a confession, absolution through speech as in Clegg's case. The reader is put in the position of receiving this guilty man's testimony and re-enacting his pursuit of the fantasies of the masque. These elements of narrative seduction become increasingly ambiguous as the book develops.

Urfe's masculine identity can be directly related to his time. Fowles has said that 'he was meant to be a typical inauthentic man of the 1945-50 period',[5] and Urfe himself feels that Conchis was interested in him for 'some syndrome I exhibited, some category I filled. I was not interesting in myself, but only as an example.' (*M*, p.81) At the trial he is said to typify what Conchis described in his supposed book *The Midcentury Predicament*, the failed rebel who has adopted 'a mask of cynicism that cannot hide [his] more or less paranoiac sense of having been betrayed by life' (*M*, p.433). That this is directly linked to Urfe's form of masculinity is left in no doubt by the terms of the psychoanalytical report delivered during the trial itself.

Fowles has done his best in his recorded statements to expose this scene as a deliberate pastiche. He told James Campbell in 1974, 'that trial scene at the time was written as a send-up of psychology—I put in every piece of psychological jargon I could find.'[6] And in the book itself it is explained as merely one more of Conchis' manipulative fantasies (*M*, p.498). But the 'Freudian jargon' (*M*, p.460), however comical, serves a significant enough purpose by explaining Urfe's behaviour primarily in terms of his psychology as a man. And the seriousness of that is suggested by the analogy made between his choice not to cat-whip Lily and Conchis' earlier choice not to batter the Greek resistance fighters to death with a German sub-machine gun during the war (*M*, p.440).

Certainly the psychoanalytical exposé of Urfe begins humorously enough: when in exasperation at his predicament, he gives his inquisitors a double V-sign, Lily explains that 'we may suppose a castration motive in the insult, a desire to degrade and humiliate the male rival' (*M*, p.430). The report itself is couched in absurdly pseudo-Freudian terms, all of which have their resonances in Urfe's case. Having been congratulated on the 'normality' of his responses to their tests and trials, he is treated to a description of his 'condition', what he himself earlier called his 'technique':

> The subject has preyed sexually and emotionally on a number of young women. His method, according to Doctor Maxwell, is to stress and exhibit his loneliness and unhappiness—in short, to play the little boy in search of the lost mother. He thereby arouses repressed maternal instincts in his victims which he then proceeds to exploit with the semi-incestuous ruthlessness of this type. (*M*, pp.431-2)

Urfe is an emotional parasite, fundamentally narcissistic, an immature egocentric dedicated to self-gratification and playing out manipulative roles to achieve it. 'The most significant feature of his life-style', the report states, 'is negative: its lack of social content':

> The motives for this attitude spring from an only partly resolved Oedipal complex. The subject shows characteristic symptoms of mingled fear and resentment of authority, especially male authority and the usual accompanying basic syndrome: an ambivalent attitude towards women, in which they are seen both as desired objects and as objects which have betrayed him, and therefore merit his revenge and counterbetrayal. (*M*, p.431)

Central to this, the report explains to Urfe, is his family background, 'a troubled period of separation from the maternal breast, possibly due to the exigences of the military career of the subject's father, and a very early identification of the father, or male, as separator—a role which Doctor Conchis adopted in our experiment.' (*M*, p.431) This has led him into a 'repetition compulsion' (*M*, p.432), in the form of repeated affairs and artistic delusions of grandeur, which are the 'normal cultural life-pattern of the type' (*M*, p.433). To this is added an appendix, suggesting that 'breast-fixated men like the subject will become the norm' in the amoral, permissive era of consumer capitalism envisaged by Professor Ciardi (*M*, p.434). Meanwhile, Doctor Maxwell (Lily) excuses Urfe somewhat by arguing that 'the subject's selfishness and social inadequacy have been determined by his past, and any report which we communicate to him should make it clear that his personality deficiencies are due to circumstances outside his command.' (*M*, pp.434-5)

Brought to account in this way, Urfe's trial shows him up to himself as the typical product of that post-war 'crisis of masculinity' identified by Andrew Tolson among others in terms very close to those Fowles uses here.[7] And for all its spoof elements, the report embodies many of the features of a valid psychoanalytical explanation of the social construction of male models and roles of the time. Fowles's dismissiveness about this scene of indictment and castigation is, one suspects, partly defensive; for there is a sense—and we shall see others—in which it and *The Magus* is general tell of a personally felt sense of guilt on his part as a male. Thus, one fascinating point about the report is its proximity to the obsessive male novelist syndrome which Fowles identifies in his 'Hardy and the Hag' essay as at the root of his own creative drive, the compulsively compensatory mother loss which *The Collector* and now *The Magus* see lying behind the male Jekyll-and-Hyde schizophrenia about women. The manipulative fantasies of the male novelist are themselves being put on trial as forms of male power in a self-consciously tongue-in-cheek way and Urfe is representative of the interaction between the male desire to control and to project fantasies in both respects as ordinary man and as surrogate male novelist.

Urfe's inadequacies in relationships and his compensatory employment of power are linked to a specific social background in other ways. Urfe told Conchis that his sense of defeat and pessimism was 'not all me. It's in the age. In all my generation.' (*M*, p.132) At Oxford, he was 'too green to know that all cynicism masks a failure to cope—an impotence, in short' (*M*, p.12). His negative attitudes stemmed, he now realises, from the patriarchal Victorian values of his middle-class family. The repressive regime of his father, the public school and military service (*M*, pp.10-11) are the roots of his emotionally contradictory identity. It is the same repressed male English persona which Miranda saw in Piers and which Urfe sees writ large in Mitford: 'I disliked Mitford because he was crass and mean, but even more because he was a caricature, an extension, of certain qualities in myself; he had on his skin, visible, the carcinoma I nursed inside me.' (*M*, p.532) Urfe now sees his family's lack of real humanity, 'Yet still that home, those years, governed me; I had to repress the natural response' and typically he feels that in this it is he who is to be pitied: 'They had been wrong, at the trial. It was not that I preyed on girls; but the fact that my only access to normal humanity, to social decency, to any openness of heart, lay through girls, preyed on me. It was in that that I was the real victim.' (*M*, p.525)

This suggests that Urfe was and, if the self-pity is anything to go by, still is acting out the social roles available from the script of masculinity according to the legacy of his own upbringing—the family, the public school, the army. Fowles allows for this view by deploying narrative devices which, as in *The Collector*, call attention to the fictionality of the book and thus to the constructed nature of its illusion. He shows Urfe scripting his life according to socially current models. At Oxford, he and his friends 'called a certain kind of inconsequential behaviour "existentialist". Less enlightened people would have called it capricious or just plain selfish; but we didn't realize that the heroes, or anti-heroes, of the French existentialist novels we read were not supposed to be realistic. We tried to imitate them, mistaking metaphorical descriptions of complex modes of feeling for straightforward prescriptions of behaviour.' (*M*, p.12) More humorously, halfway through the book Fowles has Urfe say to Alison during the scene in the Athens hotel, 'This experience. It's like being halfway through a book. I can't just throw it in the dustbin.' (*M*, p.243)

This self-consciousness serves a number of functions, but specifically it points to the playing out of social ideology as a form of false or limited consciousness. In fiction characters literally are their roles and have no life apart from them. Drawing attention to this and, as Fowles does, giving an illusion of possible choice or escape serves to call the lived roles of social ideology into question. Urfe's case relates this directly to his male identity and his egocentric perception of the world as focusing on him:

> all my life I had tried to turn life into fiction, to hold reality away; always I had acted as if a third person was watching and listening and giving me marks for good or bad behaviour—a god like a novelist, to whom I turned, like a character with the power to please, the sensitivity to feel slighted, the ability to adapt himself to whatever he believed the novelist-god wanted. This leechlike variation of the super-ego I had created myself, fostered myself, and because of it I had always been incapable of acting freely. It was not my defence; but my despot. (*M*, p.460)

Urfe's narcissism is most fully displayed in the masque which shows him both scripting and being scripted by fantasies which he projects and which control him. For this reason Fowles also invokes the patterns of archetypal myth and, as in *The Collector*, grounds the book in previous fictions, *The Tempest* again being one obvious example. These show Urfe trapped by the legacy of male fantasies and power, and at the same time actively reimposing those fictions as forms of control.

Like Clegg then, Urfe is the victim as much as the perpetrator of male ideology; but as perpetrator, he has the crucial advantage over the victims of his sexual gamesmanship. The masque and the trial are the means by which Fowles shows the manipulator being manipulated. His sexual insecurity is exposed by playing out his desires in ways which challenge his dominant position, laying bare the myths of masculinity which he embodies. But the book does so in ways which are redolent with the very myths it focuses on. We can see this contradiction at work in a number of aspects of the narrative, specifically the figure of Conchis, the masque and the aftermath of the trial. All of them make an indictment of male behaviour whose bitterness and guilt are clear, but whose function is ambivalent.

This is apparent in the figure of Conchis. He is the agency through which Urfe is to be 'disintoxicated' of his love of power over people and his fantasies about women. There are two problems to take note of. One is a problem which faces Fowles himself as author. While purveying an ethic of freedom and choice, Conchis is effectively a manipulative dictator, a sublime patriarch, the surrogate male 'separator' of the report (*M*, p.431). In an early review, Bill Byrom expressed an unease at the way Urfe is used in the godgame: 'That a group of individuals should conspire to baffle another person until he comes to an improved sense of himself, is to put ends before means in a totalitarian fashion which the author seems to condone... Pervading the book, there is a brutality not wholly acknowledged by the author.'[8] We should not take fiction literally of course, but Byrom's point does indicate a central contradiction in Fowles's work as a whole. For all his belief in the novel as 'an astounding freedom to choose', Fowles is one of the most manipulative of fictional game-players and quite ready to admit that 'when you write a book you are potentially a tyrant, you are the total dictator'.[9] Ironically enough, he seems both to embody and to betray his ethic of freedom in the very narrative strategies he adopts.

The second point is more pertinent. Originally, Fowles wanted to make the Conchis figure into a woman based upon Miss Havisham from *Great Expectations*. He says in the foreword to the revised edition of the book, 'I long toyed with the notion of making Conchis a woman—an idea whose faint ghost, Miss Havisham's, remains in the figure of Mrs de Seitas.' (*MRV*, pp.6-7) Again, in an essay, he writes 'if the technical problems hadn't been so great, I should have liked to make Conchis in *The Magus* a woman. The character of Mrs de Seitas at the end of the book was simply an aspect of his character; as was Lily.'[10] And to Raman Singh Fowles confessed how he saw the connection with Dickens's novel only as an afterthought: 'I belatedly realized Conchis [in *The Magus*] is a kind of Miss Havisham figure... very interesting.'[11]

Seeing Miss Havisham as a source indicates what is quite apparent in the book itself—that, as in Miss Havisham's dealings with Pip, there is a subterranean desire for revenge on men as men involved in the 'heuristic mill' (*MRV*, p.10) which Urfe goes through. By making Conchis himself a man Fowles camouflages that point, though at the same time it allows him to make Conchis the prosecutor and judge of his own sex's power. Equally, it allows Conchis to act evasively as the surrogate for the myth that Lily and Mrs de Seitas represent—woman as repository of higher truth, the lost mother myth of which Urfe is supposedly disintoxicated through his fantasy pursuit. Making Conchis male avoids inscribing this myth into the very design of the novel, but only by contrivance. For, in effect, Conchis is the representative of the 'female' values which are Fowles's touchstone, and which are used so ambiguously to expose male power and idealisation.

We can see this paradoxical process at work in one of the book's most powerful and direct indictments of male 'values' and the masculine ideology of power. It comes in chapter 53 when Conchis describes to Urfe the atrocities committed by the Nazi commandant, Wimmel. It makes explicit a connection between masculinity, war and a social death-wish that Fowles hinted at in *The Collector*. Having graphically evoked the horrors of Wimmel's fascist command, Conchis explains his own sense of shame:

> 'Because these events could have taken place only in a world where man considered himself superior to woman. In what the Americans call "a man's world". That is, a world governed by brute force, humourless arrogance, illusory prestige, and primeval stupidity.' He stared at the screen. 'Men love war because it allows them to look serious. Because it is the one thing that stops women laughing at them. In it they can reduce women to the status of objects. That is the great distinction between the sexes. Men see objects, women see the relationship between objects. Whether the objects need each other, love each other, match each other. It is an extra dimension of feeling that we men are without and one that makes war abhorrent to all real women—and absurd. I will tell you what war is. War is a psychosis caused by an inability to see relationships. Our relationship with our fellow-men. Our relationship with our economic and historical situation. And above all our relationship to nothingness, to death. (*M*, p.352)

The 'craving to risk death' is, Conchis tells Urfe, a social malaise, 'our last great perversion' (*M*, p.114), the manifestation of a society dominated by masculine power. He berates Urfe personally for his anti-life attitudes on a number of occasions: 'you are sick, my young friend. You live by death. Not by life.' (*M*, p.377) For Conchis, Urfe's view of life was 'a disaster. So defeated. So pessimistic.' (*M*, p.132) It is an expression at the level of the individual of the social negativity enacted by men in war.

We can notice two points about this. Firstly, Conchis' critique of war is done in terms of Fowles's analysis of the 'male' and 'female' principles of *The Aristos*. The truth for which Urfe quests, then, is embodied in values associated with the 'female' principle which Conchis upholds. It is to this speech by Conchis that Urfe returns at the very end of the book when he tries to convince Alison that he is in fact capable of changing (*M*, p.568). His quest is to be 'feminised' out of his masculine behaviour.

The second point is a broader one. By bringing in the war episode in this way, Fowles indicates a connection between male power in personal terms and in terms of the wider social processes of which war is a manifestation. Amid the fantastical ordeals in which Urfe and the reader are caught up, *The Magus* contains Fowles's most angry impeachment of men as warmongers, specifically in Conchis' accounts of Neuve Chapelle and the village massacre. The connection and its contemporary relevance are made explicit in the 'Foreword' to the revised version of the book, in which Fowles expresses the wish that 'there were some super-Conchis who could put the Arabs and Israelis, or the Ulster Catholics and Protestants, through the same heuristic mill as Nicholas' in order to bring about the 'destruction of such illusions' concerning 'absolute knowledge and absolute power' (*MRV*, p.10).

This suggests that Fowles sees war as manifesting the dangerous armoury of male power in its most overt form—what he has called, in an article on the phenomenon of the Falklands war, 'that lethal blend of machismo, braggadocio and hypertrophic sense of honour'[12] underpinning patriarchal society. But for all the sharpness with which this judgement is posed in *The Magus*, finally it is subsumed in the personalised quest of the one character, Urfe, as part of his search for redemption. Framing the book in this way tends to mean that the wider social issues are seen as an analogy for the individual behaviour of Urfe and this inevitably suggests that such social processes are the effects of individual men writ large, rather than of men as a class. As a result, Fowles puts himself in the position of locating the possibilities for change simply at the level of the individual consciousness, rather than seeing them in wider political terms as well. The limits of this are engraven into the figure of Conchis himself: 'He was like a man who wanted to change all; and could not; so burned with his impotence; and only me, an infinitely small microcosm, to convert or detest.' (*M*, p.377) The problems involved in such a position emerge as Fowles takes us through the circular maze of Urfe's attempts to learn from his experiences. A sense of impasse is built into the very structure of the book.

As with the figure of Conchis, Urfe's quest through the masque is suffused with elements of contradiction indicative of Fowles's ambiguousness in his treatment of masculinity in *The Magus*. The various fantasies which the masque enacts are essentially projections of Urfe's male ego. The myths of war, honour, and above all women—women as a solution, 'that dream of two complementary, compliant women' (*M*, p.329), 'the charms of a *ménage à trois*' (*M*, p.280)—are all exposed and demystified, Urfe's display of stereotypical attitudes being held up by himself as a test case of male reactions. Much of the investigation is done through Lily and Rose, the twins whose archetypal names embody that central mythic dualism of male ideology, the pure woman and the scarlet woman. In the words of an American critic, 'Lily is a cipher, a woman who never existed, who was invented, as Ferdinand created a false Miranda, solely to cater to masculine fantasies about the nature of the ideal woman.'[13]

Notably, all the previous victims of Conchis' godgame have been men and all of them seem to have undergone an experience of humiliation. Urfe is thoroughly bewildered by the changing roles Lily and Rose adopt, but the fundamental point to note is his role as the central subject, 'reading' the ambiguous action of the masque as a reflection of his own desires.

Mrs de Seitas later tells him 'My daughters were nothing but a personification of your own selfishness' and, when he justifies himself by saying that he happened 'to fall in love with one of them' her reply leaves us in no doubt about the connection between this book and Fowles's first: 'As an unscrupulous collector falls in love with a painting he wants. And will do anything to get.' (*M*, p.519) His fantasies are part of a mythology of power and possession, which the masque reflects back as such. So, once it is under way, Urfe has 'the strangest feeling... of having entered a myth; a knowledge of what it was like physically, moment by moment, to have been young and ancient, a Ulysses on his way to meet Circe, a Theseus on his journey to Crete, an Oedipus still searching for his destiny.' (*M*, p.143) From the moment when he presumes that Conchis' mysterious woman

companion would have 'tried to catch a glimpse of me' (*M*, p.79),
he unhesitatingly assumes that all that happens is for his benefit,
that Lily will undoubtedly fall in love with him, and that he has
unfailing command of the games he plays. He never once
considers the self-imposing limits of his view of the world, and the
one role he never imagines Lily as capable of playing is her 'real'
one, completely outside the compass of his male imperatives.
Urfe's masculine blindness is writ large in the masque and Fowles
uses it to probe the mythologies he projects and suffers from:

> After all, it was a masque, and I wanted, or after a very short while began to
> want, to play my part. I found something a shade patronizing in her
> attitude, and I interpreted it as an attempt to upstage me; perhaps to test me,
> to see if I was worth playing against... In any case, I found her far too pretty,
> both in repose and in action (or acting), to care. I thought of myself as a
> connoisseur of girls' good looks; and I knew that this was one to judge all
> others by. (*M*, p.154)

It is part of Urfe's own presumptuously patronising attitude that
he assumes behind Lily's various guises an *Ur*-Lily whose role
must necessarily relate directly to his needs, an object to be
possessed for his benefit. What fascinates Urfe about Lily is her
enigmatic nature, her unpredictable, changeable ambiguousness,
an enigma to which he assumes he has the solution. In effect, he is
correct since it is an enigma he invents:

> Lily gave strongly the impression that she was playing with me—amusing
> herself as much as acting a role at Conchis's command. But all games, even
> the most literal, between a man and a woman are implicitly sexual; and I
> was clearly meant to feel that. If it was her job to seduce me, I should be
> seduced. I couldn't do anything about it. I was a sensualist. I wanted to be
> seduced (*M*, p.186)

> I said after a few moments, 'You're trying—very successfully—to
> captivate me. Why?'
> She made no attempt this time to be offended. One realized progress more
> by omissions than anything else; by pretences dropped.
> 'Am I?'
> 'Yes.'
> She picked up the mask and held it like a yashmak again.
> 'I am Astarte, mother of mystery.' The piquant grey-violet eyes dilated,
> and I had to laugh.
> I said, very gently, 'Buffoon.'

The eyes blazed. 'Blasphemy, O foolish mortal!' (*M*, p.189)

What he sees as an enigmatic element in Lily intrigues Urfe as he repeatedly tries to contain it, despite warnings from both Conchis and Lily. It is simultaneously a quest and a power battle, best won in his terms through typically manipulative manoeuvres. His problem is of becoming caught up in his own illusions. At the point when he supposes Lily to have abandoned all pretence and have revealed her real self, Urfe caresses her face 'with a timidity I felt but would in any case have simulated' (*M*, p.306). He shows his attempts to impose a recognisable script on each situation that he meets and, equally, his opportunistic inclination for self-indulgence. In chapter 45 we learn how he meets Lily and she kisses him with a passion that seems to confirm his illusions: 'I thought I finally knew her. She had abandoned all pretence'. (*M*, p.275) By a typical twist of the plot, his fantasies are exposed for what they are by his realisation that it is not Lily but her twin sister Rose who has just kissed him. Not to be put out, Urfe ignores this blatant contradiction of his new-found certitude and decides to make the most of it with Rose: 'I smiled, to show her I was totally unfooled; but prepared to play a part in this new variation.' (*M*, p.277) Urfe's pursuit of Lily as the authentic ideal woman is exactly that—the pursuit of an idea, the product of male desire, appropriate to male needs but bearing no relation to actual circumstances or people, and merely the other side of his Don Juanism. When Lily says 'You don't know how sick I am of being a figure of mystery', Urfe's response is 'Mystery becomes you.' (*M*, p.291)

The real nature of Urfe's idealisation is exposed in the contrast between his fantasies of Lily and his treatment of Alison during the Athens sequence. Initially, she serves as an insurance in the event of his hopes on Phraxos foundering. Before meeting Lily, he has already begun to regenerate illusions about Alison as a 'standard to go by' and his possible 'protector' (*M*, p.99). He wishes at one point that she, or her equivalent, were there to share his experiences at Bourani (*M*, p.117), but when she actually writes to him he no longer wants that, having met Lily. His fantasies about her, however, are still easily displaced by erotic fantasies about

Alison, 'of the dirty weekend pleasures of having her in some Athens hotel bedroom; of birds in the hand being worth more than birds in the bush' (*M*, p.144). Writing to her, he adopts a pose which allows a double indemnity: the letter has 'the right balance between regretful practicality and yet sufficient affection and desire for her still to want to climb into bed if I got half a chance' (*M*, p.144). She was, he admits later, 'something that could be used if nothing better turned up' (*M*, p.217). The blatancy of this is only outdone by Urfe's subsequent intrigues. In rapid succession, he lies to Lily about 'this other girl' (*M*, p.191), to Conchis (*M*, p.206) and, most blatantly, to Alison herself about his lack of interest in Lily (*M*, p.241) and his fake syphilis, to 'make her sorry for me *and* make her keep at arm's length' (*M*, p.217).

The function of his re-encounter with Alison is multiple. At its centre, it serves to expose his illusions and manipulations, providing a counterpart in terms of 'real' experience to the 'disintoxication' (*M*, p.442) after the trial scene. It shows Urfe to be totally incapable of registering people's needs outside his own terms. Self-seduced by her presence despite his resolutions, he soon began to feel 'The lone wolf was a myth' (*M*, p.231), and 'I must tell her the truth; and not as a confession, but as a means of letting her see the truth, that my real disease was not something curable like syphilis, but far more banal, and far more terrible, a congenital promiscuity.' (*M*, p.235) That this 'truth' is a complete misnomer is shown by what subsequently occurs: having made love—as he admits 'not sex, but love' (*M*, p.240)—with an infallible sense of timing, Urfe uses that moment to tell Alison about Bourani and Lily in the totally egocentric belief that she would understand and accept it: 'I had chosen the worst of all possible moments to be honest, and like most people who have spent much of their adult life being emotionally dishonest, I overcalculated the sympathy a final being honest would bring.' (*M*, p.240) His motive for being 'honest' was 'love, that need to be naked... that need to be understood' (*M*, p.240). As always, Urfe's desire to gain sympathy outweighs his ability to sympathise. The emotional dishonesty of this confession can be seen as part of his strategies of power, confession being central to his use of the women in his life as absolvers of his guilt. What follows serves to explode the male myth of romantic idealisation, to reveal this power at its most overt and unmediated.

When Alison's lack of understanding becomes apparent Urfe's 'solution' is 'to get her back into the hotel, make love to her, prove to her through the loins that I did love her. . . and why not, let her see that I might be worth suffering, just as I was and always would be' (*M*, p.243). The resumed attempt to explain infuriates Alison and her explosion lays bare the true nature of Urfe's romantic fantasies:

> I think you're so blind you probably don't even know you don't love me. You don't even know you're a filthy selfish bastard who can't, can't like being impotent, can't *ever* think of anything except number one. Because nothing can hurt you, Nicko. Deep down, where it counts. You've built your life so that nothing can ever reach you. So whatever you do you can say, I couldn't help it. You can't lose. You can always have your next adventure. Your next bloody affaire. . . All that mystery balls. You think I fall for that? There's some girl on your island and you want to lay her. That's all. But of course that's nasty, that's crude. So you tart it up. As usual. Tart it up so it makes you seem the innocent one, the great intellectual who must have his experience. Always both ways. Always cake and eat it. Always—(*M*, p.245)

Her accusations of emotional impotency, of fear of feeling, of the schizophrenia about sex and love that we saw in Clegg, all indict Urfe, as a man, for moral bankruptcy; and that it *is* as a man is demonstrated by what happens next: he physically attacks Alison by trying to force her to kiss him, and finally slaps her face.

This whole episode is centrally important in a number of ways, not least because, along with Conchis' speech on war and the report in the trial scene, it provides a key arraignment of masculine behaviour which, in its effects, comes nearest to the bone of any in the book. It also has a structural importance, since the slap in the face recurs at the very end of the novel, seeming to confirm that this is Urfe 'as I was and always would be' (*M*, p.243). But it also points an accusing finger at the male novelist's own obsessional fantasies about mystery women, Fowles's ambiguous abdication of social responsibility for 'that mystery balls'.

The sense that Urfe is ensnared in a cycle of repetitions begins to be made concrete. He shows up his reactions to Alison's departure in terms identical to those in London at the beginning of the book. He admits to a 'secret relief' on finding her gone (*M*, p.248), and congratulates himself in hardened 'lone wolf' fashion in the bar over a stiff drink: 'I drank a mouthful neat, and made a sort of bitter inner toast. I had chosen my own way; the difficult, hazardous, poetic way; all on number one.' (*M*, p.249) He even repeats the stagey note, asking Alison to write back, since 'It's so likely that one day I shall need you terribly, I shall come crawling to you, and you can have all the revenge you want then.' His comment on the letter is 'I thought it a good letter; the only conscious exaggeration was in the last sentence.' (*M*, p.250)

At this point Urfe's self-exposure of his past behaviour shows it reaching a point of crisis in which all the relevant contradictions emerge as the masque intensifies and his quest for the 'real' Lily becomes more fraught. He admits that he felt increasingly as if he were part of a myth, like Theseus in the maze aware that 'somewhere in the darkness Ariadne waited; and the Minotaur' (*M*, p.274), but this fabulous beauty and her beast exist only in the labyrinth of his own psyche.

Having learnt of Alison's supposed suicide, Urfe realises his responsibility for his 'monstrous crime', for having 'imposed the role I needed from Alison on her real self' (*M*, p.341). That does not prevent him from doing exactly the same with Lily. She now 'became a total necessity. Not only marriage with her, but confession *to* her.' (*M*, p.341) Urfe's guilt is plainly shown as evasively self-indulgent, even at this point: Alison's death heightens the 'hope of Julie', Lily's 'real' name; and by a 'sinister elision' he slips 'from true remorse... to disguised self-forgiveness' as he looks forward to absolution from Julie–Lily: 'I was still determined to tell Julie, but at the right time and place, when the exchange rate between confession and the sympathy it evoked looked likely to be high.' (*M*, pp.342-3)

Significantly, it is at this point in Urfe's machinations that Fowles locates Conchis' critique of male power in war, just prior to the description of Wimmel's atrocities. The structural link is important since we have just been told of Urfe at his most personally brutal and his most deludedly idealistic. The connection between male ideology and fascism is made through his failure to see relationships—he merely sees stereotypes of the ego. Wimmel is an ultra-manipulator who imposed 'chaos on order' (*M*, p.367) with self-knowledge, in pursuit of sheer power. Urfe, unlike Wimmel, is the victim of his own delusions but they share the same desire to manipulate and control. The masque provided a series of such object lessons for Urfe, analogies for his personal behaviour. Foulkes is a paedophile and a victim of the law (*M*, p.126); de Deukans is a misogynistical collector (*M*, p.160); Julie has been 'interfered with' as a child, so that 'with even the nicest men, men like you—I can't help suspecting that they're just using me.' (*M*, p.306) In one form or another, all these are analogues for male power politics of the kind Urfe continues to indulge in.

One crucial problem with the exposé provided by the masque, however, is that the book itself acts to seduce the reader—perhaps we should specify the male reader—into an imaginary pursuit of the very fantasies it exposes. It repeatedly suggests the promise of imaginative access to women figures, real or fantastic, who are part of the basic idea of the book as Fowles has crucially described it—'a secret world, whose penetration involved ordeal and whose final reward was self-knowledge'.[14] This 'penetration' is both fulfilled and frustrated with an effect which is both tantalising and titillating.

This teasing note is written into the book in diverse ways. It is there in the form of Urfe's obsessively sexual speculations, his continual state of erotic suggestibility, which is simultaneously shown to be deluded fantasy and effectively used upon the reader: 'It was ridiculous to build so much on the sound of quick footsteps, the merest glimpse of a glimpse of a white shape.' (*M*, p.123) 'Perhaps you are teasing yourself' (*M*, p.158), Lily tells Urfe, but there is no doubt that the book does so with the reader. It is also there in the continual sexual awareness afforded by the art objects in Conchis' house—the phallic clock (*M*, p.92), the priapus statue with its enormous erect penis (*M*, p.74), the erotic literature Conchis gives Urfe (*M*, pp.90, 150). It is present in Conchis' story of the beautiful Lily Montgomery whom he loved and lost as a young man, with all its romantic nostalgia for this mysterious woman who is then made 'real' for Urfe (*M*, pp.103-4). But most of all, it is written into the very narrative structure of the book, Fowles's favourite motif of the quest-pursuit whose twists of plot lead the reader on the same dance as Urfe and with the same result, a disintoxication and a renewal of primary male sexual fantasies.

When Urfe tells Conchis that he is 'in love' with Lily, Conchis' response is 'This is all I have tried to avoid in my theatre. Now it *is* theatre—make-believe and artifice.' (*M*, p.380) The disintoxication Urfe goes through was designed to sober him up about himself. The crucial chapters are 58-9 and they are among the most heavily revised in the 1977 version of the book. In both versions, however, Urfe undergoes a symbolic castration in which he is rendered powerless and brought face to face with the banal realities of his actions.

In the original edition, the sequence describing Urfe's attempt to make love to Julie and the revelation of her duplicity is done with a violence whose effect is to absolutely humiliate Urfe at the basic sexual level, showing him as pathetically inadequate and dangerous. There is no sympathetic listening by Julie as he unburdens his conscience about Alison, as in the later version. Instead, the anticipated romantic-erotic encounter turns into a humiliating frustrating 'sexual guessing-game' with Julie posing now as a slave, now as Eve (*M*, p.410). Urfe, with a contraceptive installed over his erect penis, chases her round the room trying desperately to get her in his power. He finally pleads 'Julie. Come on. For Chist's sake', more out of 'despair than pleasure'. She forces him to admit 'I'm dying for you' at which moment, with a drama not matched by the later version, the truth is revealed:

'Julie?'
I saw her pale figure against the faint rectangle; watching me for a moment. Her right hand reached sideways.
She spoke. The strongest voice; as hard as glass.
'There is no Julie.' (*M*, p.411)

The suddenness with which Urfe's illusions collapse links with the radical inversion of the standard male-female power structure to bring about an important synthesis of the two themes.

By having Lily–Julie take the upper hand and shatter Urfe's fantasies at the same time, Fowles lays the ground for the depiction of Urfe's subsequently violent reaction in a way which is more coherent than in the later edition. The sudden exposure to vulnerability and the threat to his power reveal in Urfe the underlying premise on which his idealising love is based, effective superiority and control. From being his desired ideal, Urfe tells us, Lily now became 'Circe' (*M*, p.416), the dangerous woman with power over men, a 'prostitute' who had brought about 'the vile and unforgivable, the ultimate betrayal, of me, of all finer instincts' (*M*, p.415). Like Clegg's, his reaction is a desire to reassert his power through violence and denigration: 'Only one thing could ever give me relief. Some equal humiliation of Lily. It made me furious that I had not been more violent with her before.' (*M*, p.417) At the same time, he admits to feeling thoroughly insecure in the face of Lily's autonomy. He recalls Conchis' description of Wimmel's torture room with 'a man lying on his back on the table; symbolically castrated'; and when Lily returns to look at him, she seems like 'a woman surgeon who had just performed a difficult operation successfully. Peeling off the rubber gloves; surveying the suture.' (*M*, p.412)

One of Fowles's stated aims in revising *The Magus* was that it 'wasn't quite erotic enough' in the original version.[15] The revisions of this section were presumably aimed at overcoming this apparent deficiency. The turnabout of victimizer into victim is done more gently and with a direct fulfilment of the sexual encounter. Julie maintains the illusion of a romantic connection, playing the role of ultimately sympathetic and seductively submissive woman to the full. Even the disenchantment is done sympathetically, as if she were regretful that the dream must be shattered, almost apologetic for Urfe's ordeal. As a result, the subsequent disorientation as Urfe is taken for the trial comes as a dramatic plot-switch, but without the bite of the first version. Equally, the increased 'erotic' element makes the paradoxical mixture of fantasised indulgence and flagellatory guilt, in the form of the ensuing trial, even more obvious.

The trial offers Urfe the chance to learn *not* to wield power, to almost castrate himself. The 'viciously cruel vivisection of the mind' (*M*, p.416) that he feels himself to be undergoing forces on him a voluntary abdication of power whose outcome is crucial in trying finally to assess the extent to which, in this book, Fowles could see the possibility for change in Urfe and in men in general. The very paradox of being forced into voluntary abdication indicates the extent of the problem and it is this that the rest of the book explores.

After the exposé of the report which effectively explains Urfe's behaviour both to himself and to the reader, the temptation to whip Lily in revenge tests how much he has understood of the hidden commandment behind his ordeals—the imperative which Mrs de Seitas later makes clear: '*Thou shalt not commit pain.*' (*M*, p.556) Urfe realised, he tells us, that his 'freedom', like Conchis' in the war, lay 'in not striking, whatever the cost' (*M*, p.440). But the disintoxication with power is designed to go deeper to the very sexual foundation of his male identity. The pornographic movie and the live copulation scene between Lily and Joe tackle Urfe at the roots of his insecurities. But their function in the novel is contradictory. The sexual quest is fulfilled before Urfe's eyes and those of the voyeuristic reader, and the effect on Urfe is to disenchant him of Lily in a quite perverse way. He suddenly grasps the original behind her various roles, the 'seed of all betrayal' (*M*, p.451), a phrase significantly cut from the 1977 version: 'I suddenly knew her real name, behind the masks of Lily, of Julie, of Artemis, of the doctor, of Desdemona. . . I knew her real name. I did not forgive, if anything I felt more rage. But I knew her real name.' (*M*, pp.451-2) We are not told what that name is, but given that Urfe's attendant had been Adam, we can hazard a guess. The root of Urfe's fear and misogyny, his sense of betrayal, is traced to that most fundamentally patriarchal of myths, the fall of man for which Eve, the fatal woman, was made responsible. Ignoring the psychological explanation of this, as given in the trial report, Urfe's revelation merely increases his desire for revenge; and it suggests that, at this stage, Fowles had seen the contradictions that might be generated in men by the imperatives of change and abdication of power.

That Urfe is fundamentally unaffected by the demystification

process is apparent in the way he resurrects Alison as an ideal of
trustworthy womanhood in contrast to Lily's duplicity—'her
normality, her reality, her predictability; her crystal core of non-
betrayal; her attachment to all that Lily was not.' (*M*, p.474)
Fowles pushes his test-case to its limits through the plot twist of
having the supposedly dead Alison reappear, as the final stage in
bringing Urfe to account. His reaction on discovering Alison to be
alive hardly bodes well. Suspecting that she must be complicit
with Conchis' manipulations he feels betrayed by her and a desire
for revenge: 'to dig or beat the truth out of her, to let her know how
vile her betrayal was. To let her know that even if she crawled
round the equator on her knees I would never forgive her... This
time I would use that cat.' (*M*, p.484-5) It is hardly the language
of a repentant convert to the 'feminine' values of tolerance and
love. Urfe's egocentricity, the root of his compulsion to gain
power, seems as fertile as ever. He resolves not to search for Alison
since he imagines that to be what 'they' want him to do in the
'script' of the masque. Almost inevitably, however, he readopts
the role of 'hunter' (*M*, p.502), playing out his final mythical role
of Orpheus searching for Eurydice in a Fowlesian parody of a
detective thriller. At the same time, he admits, he became aware
that 'a new feeling had seeded and was growing inside me, a
feeling I wanted to eradicate and couldn't, not least because I
knew the seed of it had been planted by Conchis' (*M*, p.496).

Mrs de Seitas, the 'faint ghost' of Fowles's Conchis prototype,
points the way for the still questing 'Mr Orfe' (*M*, p.510) as she
misnames him in his pursuit of his lost Eurydice, Alison, and a
supposed moral rebirth. What is notable in her explanation of
Conchis' new morality of the elect is Urfe's conservative reaction
to her ethic of sexual liberation. He feels a fearful nostalgia 'to
think of Alison in this woman's hands. As one hears of a
countryside one has loved being sold to building developers. And I
also felt left behind, abandoned again. I did not belong to this
other-planet world.' (*M*, p.522) With the familiar landscape of
male-defined sexual relations changing before his eyes, Urfe
registers his contradictory response:

> ... in one sense Mrs de Seitas had been preaching to the converted in all that she had said about a clean surgical abscission of what went on in the loins from what went on in the heart.
>
> Yet something very deep in me revolted. I could swallow her theory, but it lay queasily on my stomach. It flouted something deeper than convention and received ideas. It flouted an innate sense that I ought to find all I needed in Alison. (*M*, p.548)

Urfe can accept the liberalisation of sexual relations as long as it does not threaten a fundamentally male prerogative embodied in the present disposition of power. His innate sense that he ought to find all he needs in one woman reveals a determining of sexual arrangements in terms which reproduce a male-orientated structure. Andrew Tolson is not the only writer who has perceived that a defence of the monogamous couple and the family is often the last ditch position of the entrenched male threatened with a radical challenge to his status.[16]

The contradictions Fowles shows in action here are central to the immediate relevance of the book to his time. What we see in the ending is fundamentally a model of the reaction of contemporary men to the challenge made by those social forces during the late 1950s and 1960s which moved women towards an assertion of autonomy and the politics of feminism. Fowles shows Urfe undertaking a retrenchment and realignment of his power in order to maintain it, not simply a refusal but an inability to change or abdicate from that power. This sense of impasse comes out in the cyclical effect of the ending. What has been implicit in the quest motif—that it is compulsively repeated—emerges explicitly in what are essentially two versions in miniature of Urfe's whole predicament, his relationship with the Scottish working-class girl Jojo and his reunion with Alison.

When Mrs de Seitas gives Urfe the present of a plate, she advises him, 'I think you should get used to handling fragile objects.' (*M*, p.541) And his own anecdote of the butcher who planned to kill Marie Antoinette with an axe, but broke down in tears when confronted with her, bodes well for a new awakening in him to Conchis' message. But his treatment of Jojo merely reproduces his previous self-centred behaviour. He picks her up for companionship as a safeguard against getting involved with any other women. Because of her 'Beckett-like' appearance (*M*, p.549), she 'slipped perfectly into the role I cast her for... She fulfilled her function very well; she put off every other girl who looked at us and on my side I cultivated a sort of lunatic transferred fidelity towards her.' (*M*, p.551) Whilst he feels fairly safe from attack with her, Jojo's vulnerability, her lack of any kind of power, sexual or economic, puts her in a position of dependency the results of which are almost inevitable. When she asks him to sleep with her because she loves him, it is significantly the first time he has heard her use the verb 'to want' in the first person singular (*M*, p.553). Instead of giving her reassurance, he uses her again to confess to: 'She was the strangest priest to confess before; but not the worst. For she absolved me.' (*M*, p.555) At the same time, he realises he had transgressed the new law learnt from Conchis and Mrs de Seitas: he felt like an immature novice to whom 'Adulthood was like a mountain, and I stood at the foot of this cliff of ice, this impossible and unclimbable: *Thou shalt not commit pain.*' (*M*, p.556) The contradiction between what he now knows he ought to be and what he is registers clearly in the penultimate chapter of the book. He feels 'self-disgust' over his treatment of Jojo and at the same time resurrects the lone wolf image: 'I thought with a leap of excitement of life without Alison, of setting out into the blue again... alone, but free. Even noble' (*M*, p.558). In this frame of mind, a cross now between Clint Eastwood and Ulysses, Urfe goes to tell his landlady Kemp he is leaving. Her response is perhaps the most vitriolic indictment of Urfe's privileged middle-class male status in the book:

'Tired of slumming. Thought you would be.
...You pick up a poor little scob like that, God only knows why, then when you're sure she's head over fucking heels in love with you, you act like a real gentleman. You kick her out.'
'Look—'
'Don't kid *me*, laddie.' She sat square and inexorable. 'Go on. Run back home.'
'I haven't got a bloody home, for Christ's sake.'
'Oh yes you have. They call it the bourgeoisie.' (*M*, p.559)

Castigated as a double oppressor by this older counterpart of Jojo, Urfe goes off in a rage to pack and accidentally breaks the symbolic plate given him by Mrs de Seitas. Kemp finds him near to tears, 'the smug bastard, the broken butcher, on his knees' (*M*, p.560).

This castigation of Urfe completes a miniature re-run of the central situation of the book—the necessity for men to be brought to a point of realisation through having their power undermined. But the repeated cycle suggests what the final chapter makes clear—that for Fowles in *The Magus* there is an impasse written into masculinity itself as there is into the script of his fiction, beyond which at that point in the historical process he could not see men going.

The last chapter begins with a self-conscious authorial interjection in which 'our age' exhorts the novelist to leave this anti-hero 'at a crossroads, in a dilemma, with all to lose and only more of the same to win', since we are all 'waiting for this girl, this truth, this crystal of humanity, this reality lost through imagination, to return; and to say she returns is a lie.' (*M*, p.560) With ironic compassion, Fowles decides to give Urfe one last chance, 'ten more days'. It is ironic because what follows is again a repeat performance by Urfe, though intensified. The events of the ending literally replay central scenes and elements from the rest of the book, as if Fowles were suggesting quite logically that Urfe as a character representing the typical 'inauthentic man' of the 1950s cannot possibly escape the bounds of his role in this fiction. And by analogy this replay suggests that the myths surrounding men in terms of social ideology cannot suddenly be thrown away like an exhausted novel.

Urfe remains with Kemp, feeling that 'something in me changed. . . .Conchis' truths, especially the truth he had embodied in Lily, matured in me. Slowly I was learning to smile'. (*M*, p.561) Again this augurs a change which the reappearance of Alison in Regent's Park tests, only to find Urfe thoroughly unredeemed. The romance he had anticipated in her return—'I had imagined this scene so often; and it was always in essence a melting, a running into each other's arms' (*M*, p.564)—is distinctly lacking, since she 'was cast as Reality' (*M*, p.562). What is apparent is

Urfe's attempt to manipulate the situation to his own needs. By now, his view of Alison is supposedly without any illusions, but it remains idealising.

Except for the very last paragraph, both versions of the book agree on a generally similar pattern of events after Urfe meets Alison, though with some suggestive changes here and there. His attitude towards her is intensely contradictory: he is aggrieved, infuriated, but also he feels inadequate and in need, a feature particularly marked in the later version. His behaviour masks these deficiencies behind an aggressive exterior in a desperate attempt to regain the upper hand. He is shown basically trying to bully Alison back into the very relationship he had originally broken. In the first version, when she leaves the pavilion he goes after her 'pushing roughly past the people in my way' (M, p.562). In the second version, he does the same but gives 'chase' (MRV, p.647) and feels 'uncouth beside her': 'she had no right to re-appear like some clothes-conscious and self-possessed young middle-class wife' (MRV, p.648), and he clearly feels intimidated by her autonomy.

In what follows Urfe believes Alison to be still playing to Conchis' script, roles which he himself imposed. His attempt to re-possess her takes the same form of blatant aggression in both versions:

> I said, 'I want to make one thing clear from the start.' She said nothing. 'I forgive you that foul bloody trick you played this summer. I forgive you whatever miserable petty female vindictiveness made you decide to keep me waiting all this time.'
>
> She shrugged. A silence. Then she said, 'But?'
>
> 'But I want to know what the hell went on that day in Athens. What the hell's been going on since. And what the hell's going on now.'
>
> 'And then?'
>
> Those grey eyes; her strangeness made them colder.
>
> 'We'll see.' (M, p.563; MRV, p.648)

The flagrant egocentricity with its underlying insecurity is matched by his presumption in assuming that she has in fact come back to him. While Alison remains impassive, insisting that the masque is over, Urfe feels 'a sense of outrage, as if I was being barred from my own property.' (*M*, p.564; *MRV*, p.650) He tries every possible tactic from aggressiveness to idealising wheedling: 'You're the only person I've ever felt that about' (*M*, p.564; *MRV*, p.650, slightly changed). It becomes increasingly obvious that it is Urfe who cannot escape the scripts of sexual relations he accuses her of playing to, and that his repertoire does not contain a part that can accommodate this detached Alison who seems 'mysterious, almost a new woman' (*M*, p.565; *MRV*, p.650): 'What am I meant to do? Take you in my arms? Fall on my knees? What do they want?' (*M*, p.566; *MRV*, p.651)

From this point, the two versions begin to diverge significantly in ways which suggest that what Fowles thought appropriate to a man of the 1950s or 1960s needed modification for the man of the 1970s. But noticeably in both versions the male imperatives remain virtually intact, merely realigned. As Alison leads him into a section of the park surrounded by houses with watching windows and by a row of classical statues, Urfe suddenly has the feeling that he has been manipulated once again and that Alison is an accomplice. His reaction is to take an even more aggressive initiative to gain control of the situation and Alison. He adopts an authoritarian role, put at its most brazen in the first version. He takes her 'roughly' by the arm:

> 'Now listen.' I stood there at her shoulder, with my meanest expression. It was not a difficult part to play. That bruised face, very near to tears, but not in tears. I thought, I will get her on a bed and I will ram her. I will ram her and ram her, the cat will fall and fall, till she is full of me, possessed by me. (*M*, p.568)

The equation of sexuality with violence and power needs little comment except to say that Urfe's overt desire for control stems directly from his sense of insecurity. His reaction to the threat of not being able to control Alison is to try to take her by brute force. In the revised version, this passage is cut and his general attitude made less brutal, more solicitous. But in both he is imposing the terms of their future relationship on Alison. He presents her with an unadorned description of himself which is at least honest: he is not much of a financial prospect; if Lily walked down the path he would probably follow her, since she represents a 'type of encounter' which he cannot avoid. The other element in his self-characterisation is his recollection of Conchis' views on the differences between men's and women's views of the world, and that he now knows it is important to see relationships rather than objects: 'That's all I can offer you. The possibility that I'm beginning to see it.' (M, p.568; MRV, p.653)

In the first version, the aggressiveness of Urfe's expression makes a mockery of this; and the way in which that version ends supports the view that basically Urfe has learnt nothing. After his ultimatum, he tells Alison what he expects her to do if she is going to come with him, literally giving her a part to play and scripting a situation which he believes will allow them to escape from Conchis and the imagined masque. His scenario includes a simulated quarrel in which he will slap her face and they will leave separately, to meet later in Paddington Station waiting-room. Despite her attempts to break into this closed situation of his making, Urfe leaves Alison no real choice. She does run after him and he does slap her face. The 'savage but unavoidable slap knocking her sideways' structurally echoes the scene in the Athens bedroom halfway through the book and the implication of the re-run is that Urfe is fundamentally unchanged. Urfe's sudden realisation as Alison smiles back after being hit, 'Mocking love, yet making it', is that the masks have dropped, 'There were no watching eyes... The theatre was empty. It was not a theatre.' (M, p.570) Alison's smile and his revelation that their actions are outside the jurisdiction of the masque's scripts are equally ambiguous since he himself has just played out one archetypal male role and ends on another. His final pose is to walk off and leave her, carrying with him the perpetuation of those myths of power that serve his purpose, the lone wolf again accepting his freedom: 'Firmer than Orpheus, as firm as Alison herself, that other day of parting, not once looking back.' (M, p.570) But it is the freedom of the oppressor rather than the oppressed.

Most male critics, symptomatically enough, take the slapping of Alison's face as a gesture of existential liberation. Thus Wolfe writes that 'Urfe's slapping Alison's face instigates new life... signals new faith',[17] whilst Huffaker sees it as affirming an escape from Conchis' power: 'The slap may show her that he is no longer wearing a mask but honestly and *beyond reason* acting upon his anger, defying the godgame crew he supposes to be watching; the slap is also his way of choosing Alison, while leaving her free to choose.'[18] Both comments are remarkable pieces of critical rationalisation for a brutal action which a feminist critic would see on a quite different basis. The way in which Fowles changes this incident in the revised version suggests that his own view of it is more in line with the feminist one, as if he has rethought the implications in view of the situation of the 1970s.

The 1977 edition brings Urfe to the same point of crisis and impasse, but leaves him there with no hope of escape back into his privileged male freedom. The scenario is similar, though he is less brutal in what he says to Alison, more ready to admit that it is now he who is the solicitous one: 'You have my part now', he says, referring to their respective roles in the Athens hotel-room scene (*MRV*, p.653). He still imposes the necessity of choice on her, accusing her of 'playing to their script' when she insists she is going back to Australia; but her retort is pointed and as angry as his: 'I came back because I thought you'd changed' (*MRV*, p.654), and it is this which instigates the slap in the face. In this version, it is presented as an involuntary response by Urfe rather than calculated or deliberate; but he still justifies it as 'a necessary act; no breaking of the commandment' (*MRV*, p.654). What happens now is that Fowles holds this frame as if the two characters were slowly being metamorphosed into a permanent stasis. Urfe wonders whether this is not his 'last lesson and final ordeal... the task, as in *L'Astrée*, of turning lions and unicorns and magi and other mythical monsters into stone statues.' (*MRV*, p.655) His pose becomes explicit as a banal stereotype of male behaviour from which, we are told, the other strollers on the park walk away as the reader might, 'as if this trivial bit of masculine brutality, the promised scene, had lost their interest also' (*MRV*, p.655). And Alison's response is not to smile but to tell Urfe she hates him, expressing in her tone 'hatred, pain, every female resentment since time began' (*MRV*, p.655). Urfe is finally cast as repentant petitioner rather than devil-may-care individualist. His final words indicate a guilt-ridden desperation as he struggles to come to terms with Alison's self-sufficiency and the 'something' in her 'I had never seen, or always feared to see'. He urges her that he now accepts her view of 'love', but in a manner which holds little hope for the future: '"I understand that word now, Alison. Your word." Still she waited, face hidden in her hands, like someone being told of a tragic loss. "You can't hate someone who's really on his knees. Who'll never be more than half a human being without you."' (*MRV*, p.655)

Urfe never gets an answer, for Fowles freezes the action as a cinema director might, leaving the two characters in this antithetical stance in which 'All waits, suspended' (*MRV*, p.656), like stone statues themselves. Their posture is the emblem of a deadlock increasingly apparent in the 1970s between the challenge of the women's movement and the incapacity, as well as lack of inclination, of men to change.

This last point is of some general significance in assessing *The Magus* as an analysis of male power. Fowles institutes a penetrating, though thoroughly ambiguous, critique of masculinity showing the interconnections between its action on the personal and wider social levels. Urfe's 'trivial little bit of masculine brutality' is registered in both versions as a form of power politics common to male behaviour in sexual relations as in warfare. Urfe's quest is posed as an attempted initiation into the way women view the world as made up of relationships rather than objects, with the implication that life demands understanding, tolerance and love rather than possession, control and power. Thus, particularly in the revised version, the drive of the book suggests that unless men are prepared to be 'feminised', to stop hiding their vulnerability behind the masks and effects of power, then the world will go on being one in which events like the two world wars and Urfe's sexual manipulations take place.

The problem with this is that it is essentially, one might say necessarily, a moral argument rather than a political one. It does nothing to tackle the problem of male power as a political reality, because it locates any process of change in men at the level of the individual being educated into a new awareness. Nor does it tackle the inevitable problem of the reluctance, not to say resistance, of men as individuals and as a social class voluntarily to abdicate from power. This absence of a political dimension to the analysis in *The Magus* is almost inevitable given both the way Fowles has framed the narrative structure and the fact that as a male novelist he belongs to and shares the contradictions of the group he is analysing. And this comes through most obviously in that central contradiction within his work as a whole—that in order to effect his demythologising on masculinity, he invokes a reconstituted version of one of the central male myths he analyses, the ideal female as a corrective to the male. The repeated cycle of Urfe's actions in the book suggest an impasse which Fowles himself is caught in, a continued retrenchment of the male position allowing the retention of power in realigned forms.

Whether this is the only option is exactly the question which *The Magus* in its revised form leaves us with. As far as Fowles himself is concerned, the roots of his impasse in this book perhaps lie in the fact that, although published after *The Collector*, it was his earliest attempt to disengage himself from his own masculine experience in order to look at it critically. He wrote the first draft version in 1953 and, as he told Daniel Halpern in 1971, 'In a way the book was a metaphor for my own personal experience of Greece. An allegory, if you like. At least that's how it started.'[19] Of course there are a number of ways in which, as this suggests, the book might have related to Fowles's own experience. But this 'young man's first novel... this sort of adolescent book'[20] has a curiously sharp edge to its exposé of masculine violence which invites a suspicion that it bears some sense of personally felt guilt about being a man.

It is not always proper to speculate on an author's personal experience and, as an approach to a text, it can be quite misleading. Fowles has warned that the influence of Freudian and Jungian theory on an author may make it 'less and less certain nowadays that his symbols and "echoes" necessarily reveal anything of the author's private psyche', so that 'much more caution is needed on the part of the analyst'.[21] More sternly, he has understandably warned 'No writer will happily disclose the deeper biographical influences of his work, which are seldom those of outward date and occupation, and I am no exception.' (*MRV*, p.7) But in his published work, Fowles has on a number of occasions allowed glimpses of what that 'personal experience of Greece' which shaped *The Magus* might mean, and in such a way as to hint that the trial of Nicholas Urfe may have much to do with an exorcism on Fowles's part of his own sense of being complicit in the 'crime' of masculinity.

In a 'Note' published in 1973 to accompany his 1951-2 'Greek Poems', Fowles explains 'I have included them here because, together with the sense of loss I felt when various circumstances obliged me to put myself in permanent exile from Greece, they are the ground from which the novel eventually grew.'[22] When *The Magus* was published in revised form in 1977, Fowles discussed its origins in the foreword which, after mentioning the influence of the island of Spetsai and its atmosphere, includes this comment:

> No correlative whatever of my fiction, beyond the above, took place on Spetsai during my stay. What ground the events of the book have in reality came after I had returned to England. I had escaped Circe, but the withdrawal symptoms were severe. I had not then realised that loss is essential for the novelist, immensely fertile for his books, however painful to his private being. This unresolved sense of a lack, a missed opportunity, led me to graft certain dilemmas of a private situation in England on the memory of the island and its solitudes, which became increasingly for me the lost Eden, the *domaine sans nom* of Alain-Fournier. (*MRV*, p.9)

Alain-Fournier's book *Le Grand Meaulnes* has often been acknowledged by Fowles as a central influence on his own work, 'partly because there is a link with private events in my life I do not wish to discuss.'[23] Again, writing in 1978 to Robert Huffaker about the biographical fact that he met his future wife on Spetsai whilst she was married to another teacher, Fowles says 'None of that had any influence on the genesis or plot of *The Magus* whatever. I drew on the experience in one or two very general ways, in terms of mood, guilt and so on—as one draws on all experience—but in direct ways, not at all.'[24] And writing his 'Personal Note' to the translation of *Eliduc*, a text which, via 'The Ebony Tower', seems to have the same 'emotional' relationship to *The Magus* as *Le Grand Meaulnes*, Fowles writes 'the unexplained mystery, as every agnostic and novelist knows, is black proof of an ultimate shirking of creative responsibility. I have a dead weasel on my conscience; and deeper still, a dead woman.' (*ET*, p.119) *Eliduc* is a medieval romance tale of a man's betrayal of his wife for a young princess and, as Constance Hieatt puts it, 'his duplicity causes her [the princess'] death'.[25]

For all these tantalising and diverse glimpses, it is not the precise nature of the biographical background to *The Magus* that matters here, and it may well be that these individual fragments bear no relation to each other besides being John Fowles's own private *domaine*. What is of interest is the recurrent sense of personal guilt they suggest. *The Magus*, Fowles told Huffaker, was a book that 'had to be exorcised'.[26] If there is any basis for seeing the sense of guilt in the book as personally felt, perhaps this is one reason why he mystified it through his recourse to the fantastic and the enchanted. One reason for writing 'The Ebony Tower', he told Robert Robinson in 1974, was that 'In a way I wanted to demystify *The Magus*, which I think was altogether too full of mystery.'[27] And in his foreword to the poems he writes that poetry 'is normally a good deal more revealing of the writer than prose fiction. I suspect most novelists are trying to camouflage a sense of personal inadequacy in the face of real life—a sentiment that is compounded in the act of creating fiction, the fabrication of literary lies, ingenious fantasies, to hide a fundamental psychological or sociological fault of personality.' The novelist, he says, is in 'permanent flight from the mirror.'[28]

In one sense this tells us what the Hardy essay also made clear, that the male novelist's drive is part of an obsessive escapism, a schizophrenic desire to hide from life's mirror by creating in the novel a mirror for the lost sense of self and unity embodied in the mother figure. But what we also glean is a sublimated personal engagement which may go to explain why *The Magus* functions in two contrary ways at one and the same time, a confession of guilt and an extended indulgence of the very fantasies it seeks to indict or exorcise. Urfe is both a whipping-boy and a vehicle for sexual fantasy, a medium for self-flagellation but of the most ambivalent kind. In the museum scene at the end of the revised version, Mrs de Seitas asks Urfe what he thinks the purpose of evolution is: 'I shrugged. "That it allows the duds like me freedom to become a little less imperfect?"'. 'Had you done anything about it?', she asks and his answer is 'Not very much, no'. (*MRV*, p.627) Significantly enough, this revised edition of *The Magus* with its sharpened sense of the urgency for men to change appeared the year before Fowles's most contemporary and politically grounded analysis of masculinity in *Daniel Martin*. But before we examine that novel, we need to look at his exploration of the historical roots behind the contemporary forms which his male characters epitomise. This he conducted in *The French Lieutenant's Woman*.

4

The figure in the unconscious:
The French Lieutenant's Woman

When the male narrator of *The French Lieutenant's Woman* boards
the train with Charles Smithson in chapter 55, he sits observing
him with a look which is 'more than a shade disapproving, as if he
knew very well what sort of man this was (as Charles had believed
to see very well what sort of man *he* was) and did not much like the
knowledge or the species.' (*FLW*, p.347) Men as a species are very
much under scrutiny in Fowles's third published novel. It suggests
that unless the species is ready to adapt to new social conditions,
which include the emancipation of women, then, like the
aristocrat and the gentleman, certain kinds of men may find
themselves becoming evolutionary dinosaurs. Charles's 'sort of
man' is ostensibly Victorian but through him Fowles traces the
roots of present male attitudes and behaviour, suggesting as he
does so that contemporary masculinity is to be understood as part
of a historical process. Simultaneously, as the primeval battle of
male wills mentioned above indicates, the narrative of the book is
framed within a specifically male viewpoint in ways which are
highly ambiguous. All in all, one might expect the historical
distance afforded by the novel's setting to allow Fowles
detachment in his analysis of men. Instead it acts as camouflage
for the voyeur in him.

The book is partly an expiation of the Victorian past, that
legacy which so decisively shaped the men of Fowles's generation
as well as shaping his characters. Fowles told Melvyn Bragg 'I had
a little debt to settle personally with the Victorian age' in writing
The French Lieutenant's Woman.[1] For him, the Victorians are 'closer
than you may think',[2] and 'the 20th Century was already inherent

in the Victorian age'.[3] He also suggested to Bragg the central analogy between Charles's time and our own:

> for me the 20th Century was born let's say roughly between 1850 and 1870. This is when various neurosis [*sic*] begin to creep into the Victorian age. And so the heroine [of *The French Lieutenant's Woman*] of course represents at one level women's liberation[,] the beginning of the movement. And John Stuart Mill in the year in which the novel was set actually did try to you know get a vote through Parliament, to get the vote for women. He failed, of course. But that really is the beginning of sort of public, feminine emancipation.[4]

The association of women's liberation with neurosis may be more than a telling slip of the tongue. Essentially it is the male anxiety of the late 1960s at a newly-emergent female autonomy that the novel charts. It allows Fowles to explore male dilemmas which have a highly topical relevance 'to the writer's now' as he has put it.[5] To appreciate the links we need to take a brief look at the historical situation behind the book.

In *Shirley*, Charlotte Brontë's heroine complains, 'If men could see us as we really are, they would be a little amazed; but the cleverest, the acutest men are often under an illusion about women: they do not read them in a true light: they misapprehend them, both for good and evil: their good woman is a queer thing, half doll, half angel; their bad woman always a fiend.'[6] In the Parliamentary debate to which Fowles refers, John Stuart Mill spoke of the 'silent domestic revolution' taking place whereby 'women and men are, for the first time in history, really each other's companions',[7] but it is quite clear that few men at the time shared his perception or his hope. On the contrary, at the same time that forces were at work encouraging the possible liberation of women, the Victorian middle-class man's misreading of women underwent an intensification designed to keep women in the home.[8] It was an ideological strengthening of male defences against possible challenge which, as is inevitably the case, tells us far more about the Victorian male than about women. Victorian patriarchy produced its own versions of those archetypes common to male-dominated societies, the madonna-magdalen syndrome, as part of its social control. That this was a 'production' of sexual categories rather than a repression has been emphasised by a number of recent writers who see sexuality being employed within the strategies of power that maintain the dominance of certain social formations over others.[9] For Victorian women this involved living up to male imagery that both condoned and condemned their sex, the redemptive domestic angel and the outcast harlot; but it is a process which needs seeing in relation to what men were also doing to themselves. The intensification of sexual codes was equally applied to notions of masculinity to produce a model of behaviour against which men measured their own sexuality in ways as exacting as those expected of women. There is one crucial difference: the contradictions men forced themselves to live out were in the interests of maintaining their own social power as middle-class males.

Still, despite the licence allowed to men by their privilege and status, we should not underestimate what Fraser Harrison, in his book on Victorian sexuality, has called the 'psychological authority' of patriarchal codes over men's lives.[10] Restraint, guilt, a terror of economic, moral and physical bankruptcy from the ghosts of illicit sex, all played their part in enforcing heightened male standards onto the Victorian man. Marriage and the domestic ideal played a central role in the self-policing that men endured; but while the social institutions of home and family helped endorse and maintain assent to male power, they brought with them contradictions which individual men experienced as personal tensions. In his book *Sex, Politics and Society*, which examines 'The regulation of sexuality since 1800', Jeffrey Weeks has pointed out how 'Many men battled valiantly with what they conceived of as temptation and strove to live up to a higher ideal of married life',[11] often turning for help to the stream of handbooks on how to achieve male self-sufficiency. Weeks quotes the study of reproductive organs by William Acton as one example of a large number of texts which put forward 'a gospel of real manhood': Action wrote that virility is an attribute 'Much more developed in man than is that of maternity in women. Its existence, indeed, seems necessary to give a man that consciousness of his dignity, of his character as head and ruler, and of his importance, which is absolutely essential to the well-being of the family, and through it, of society itself.'[12] Given this arduous responsibility for maintaining social order through their manliness, Victorian men created a whole mythology of masculinity which was the measure of their power in their own eyes as well as the means by which it was shored up, the legacy of which we still live with. As with any structure of power, it was lived as much as an anxiety as a reassurance. The harsh constraints men imposed on themselves correlated to male economic, moral and sexual prerogatives in uneasy and demanding ways. Chastity, virility and manhood were linked to notions of duty and order in ways which promised economic success and social status for those who adhered to them, but with accompanying threats and fears about failure. Weeks demonstrates such links in the case of the obsessive concern with masturbation, as well as the cult of masculine prowess promulgated through institutions such as the growing public schools and the expanding network of male clubs. Will-power, physical strength, self-reliance, 'the new stress on games and militaristic training',[13] an accompanying imperialism, a devotion to order, duty, hierarchy, the repression of emotion and any traits associated with the heightened versions of 'femininity' of the time—all these are familiar to us now as the popular components in the imagery of masculinity, and they received specific formulation and focus in the nineteenth century as a means of social regulation, definition and organisation.

The contradictions of Victorian masculinity would have been between the clear social prestige and privilege men enjoyed and the anxieties they felt in maintaining their power and self-image. One specific anxiety developed in response to the very phenomenon Mill pinpointed—women's emancipation and its accompanying threat to male power. The feminist agitations from the 1860s onwards showed that women were capable of assuming and demanding self-determination which deeply worried orthodox male views. The emergent 'new woman' had overtones of that other woman, the *femme fatale* whom most middle-class men thought of as safely incarcerated in the brothels. It must have seemed to many men as if all the sirens and harpies they had consigned to the nether regions of their social order and their psyches were threatening to break out in vindictive retribution.

One response was the virulent anti-feminism of the later nineteenth century which asserted the domestic role of women with an aggressive dogmatism. Another response was the ambiguous portrayal of female ideals and female duplicity such as one finds in Hardy's own anxious work.

The resultant schizophrenia among men which so often projected itself in terms of seeing women as virgins, whores or both, received one remarkable exposé in the book which Fowles's narrator cites as possibly 'the best guidebook to the age' (*FLW*, p.319), R.L. Stevenson's *Dr Jekyll and Mr Hyde* (1886). As we have already noted, Stevenson's own fiction shows the male psyche as the root of that sexual duplicity about women which mirrors male fears about sexuality and power. The 'thorough and primitive duality of man'[14] which Stevenson depicts in the double personality of Jekyll was no doubt something which he felt to be part of the 'human condition' in general. Nevertheless, like Hardy's Angel Clare and Alec d'Urberville, it dramatises key tensions in Victorian masculinity whose resolution men effected through appropriating women as the imagery of their own paranoia.

In simple terms, Charles in *The French Lieutenant's Woman* embodies these contradictions to the full and in doing so he personifies a contemporary malaise of his own time and that of Fowles. The trauma Charles faces in the challenge posed by Sarah is one clearly being felt in new forms by the time Fowles published the novel and his way of telling the story is such that it answers anxiety with a realigned male fantasy in ways that are quite as contradictory as the Victorian situation it examines. To see this continuing paradox at work, let us look first at Charles as representative of the Victorian male dilemma.

Despite its title, *The French Lieutenant's Woman* is quite definitely about a man, or more precisely as we shall see, about two men. Fowles indicated as much to Melvyn Bragg when he said 'practically everyone's assumed the central character is the heroine Sarah. But for me the book was always equally about Charles.'[15] Charles represents those male assumptions which generate his fantasy of 'the French lieutenant's woman', the same patriarchal preconceptions which typecast Sarah as 'the French

Loot'n'nt's Hoer' (*FLW*, p.77), as the dairyman describes her. Charles is also the means through which those assumptions can be dissected. He is presented as characteristic of a certain type of male throughout history. He belongs to a line that extends back to the parfit knights of the Middle Ages and forwards to the modern gentleman, 'that breed we call scientists', all of whom make up a 'self-questioning, ethical elite' (*FLW*, p.256). The narrator suggests that we might not see much connection between 'the Charles of 1267 with all his newfangled French notions of chastity and chasing after Holy Grails, the Charles of 1867 with his loathing of trade and the Charles of today, a computer scientist', but we are told there is a link: 'they all rejected or reject the notion of *possession* as the purpose of life, whether it be of a woman's body, or of high profit at all costs, or of the right to dictate the speed of progress.' (*FLW*, p.257) If Charles is to be endorsed as one of this élite however—and, as we shall see, the narrator's opinions are not necessarily to be taken at face value—then it is a position which he has to earn by learning the lessons Sarah seems to offer. The transhistorical dimension suggested here is quite different to that of the male character in Günther Grass's novel *The Flounder*. In that book, the character is presented as the archetype of maleness living on throughout history and encountering the archetype of femaleness in different historical manifestations. Charles is a case-study of masculinity but in the form of a specific man living under the conditions of a specific time, 'a man struggling to overcome history' (*FLW*, p.257) but faced by an almost overwhelming pressure to conform to the general pattern laid down by patriarchal law within his society.

In this respect it is important that Charles is shown as not typical of the genus of males characteristic of his time. He does not fit in with the dominant preconceptions of male behaviour epitomised by his uncle, for example. He dislikes hunting and hunters, prefers walking to riding, and has 'a sinister fondness for spending the afternoons at Winsyatt in the library' (*FLW*, p.17). At Cambridge, he proved himself to be 'unlike most young men of his time' by actually learning something. Though he shares the general middle-class male's penchant for having a club, his excursion with some of its members to Madame Terpsichore's is more from a sense of the expected pattern of a gentleman's existence than from any anticipated enjoyment. Whilst there he finds himself unable to endure it and has to leave, with the result that his manhood feels slighted: 'He did not feel nobly decent; but as if he had swallowed an insult or funked a duel. His father had lived a life in which such evenings were a commonplace; that he could not stomach them proved he was unnatural. Where now was the travelled man of the world? Shrunk into a miserable coward.' (*FLW*, p.266)

If he is untypical, Charles is at the same time the victim of current definitions of what constitutes 'being a man'. His response is ambiguous. His struggle against the trappings of Victorian society is real enough. His early life has allowed the cultivation of the 'man of the world' persona which he adopts when he first meets Sarah, 'at ease in all his travel, his reading, his knowledge of a larger world' (*FLW*, p.107). A suitably detached attitude accompanies this privileged freedom, 'one part irony to one part convention' (*FLW*, p.18). There is also his shocking espousal of Darwinism which permits his brief camaraderie with Dr Grogan. Yet in itself, his struggle is hardly a revolt, merely the icing on his fundamental acceptance of his age, a conservatism manifest even in his challenges. His Darwinism, like his scientific pursuits, is a dilettante's pose adopted to give himself a sense of identity and worth. When, dressed the part of the Victorian palaeontologist and 'carefully equipped for his role' (*FLW*, p.45), he wanders on the seashore looking for fossils, what he sees in the strata is 'an immensely reassuring orderliness in existence... the survival of the fittest and best, *exempli gratia* Charles Smithson' (*FLW*, p.47). The palaeontological metaphor is of course ironically inverted against Charles when Sarah gives him, and puts him to, the fossil 'test', but we have already been made aware of the essentially conformist aspect of Charles's personality which he shares with the rest of this 'Adam' society.[16] On the beach he picks out a particularly large and heavy ammonite to take back for Ernestina, a labour which gives him a perverse satisfaction because of its arduousness: 'Duty, agreeable conformity to the epoch's current, raised its stern head.' (*FLW*, p.48)

Charles's central act of conformity is his proposed marriage to the aptly named Ernestina. That decision to marry is itself fraught with the paradoxical demands of Victorian masculinity in the face of respectable society's call to duty. Charles has already undergone his initiation into the male sexual schizophrenia characteristic of his age whilst in Paris, and he continues to see escape abroad as offering licence to sexual adventures (*FLW*, p.74). According to Ernestina, Sam, Charles's manservant, 'fancies himself as a Don Juan' (*FLW*, p.71) and he receives a reprimand about this from Charles for his 'past relations with the fair sex' (*FLW*, p.97); but Charles himself hardly stands free of the same accusation. Reserving Paris for his sexual exploits, in England Charles is quite ready to play the lone wolf: he 'liked pretty girls and he was not averse to leading them, and their ambitious parents, on', but 'he would sniff the bait and then turn his tail on the hidden teeth of the matrimonial traps that endangered his path' (*FLW*, p.20). This privileged position has its problem since his 'moral delicacy' increasingly leads him to abandon the weekends in Paris and as a result he 'was therefore in a state of extreme sexual frustration' (*FLW*, p.74). Hence his marriage to Ernestina presents itself as desirable sexually, the inevitable next step in his social aspirations, an unmistakable business deal and, even before the impact of Sarah, a trap.

Charles's disillusion with Ernestina is symptomatic of the contradictions he experiences as a man. His initial attraction to her is founded on a shared sense of irony and 'dryness' (*FLW*, p.72) towards social conventions. She had a quality which 'denied, very subtly but quite unmistakably, her apparent total obeisance to the great god Man', a touch which meant 'to a man like Charles she proved irresistible' (*FLW*, p.27). She takes the initiative in their relationship with a carefully timed look which 'made it clear that she made an offer; as unmistakable, in its way, as those made by the women who in the London of the time haunted the doorways round the Haymarket' (*FLW*, p.74). This air of minor revolt about Ernestina is quickly dissipated by the demands of orthodoxy: after their tiff at Mrs Poulteney's, Ernestina adopts the part of the by then less than fashionable doll-like maiden in order to reclaim Charles's affections, so much so that while 'happy to be adulated, fussed over, consulted, deferred to. What man is not?', Charles soon finds her attentions 'just a shade cloying' (*FLW*, p.100). After meeting Sarah for the second time, Charles feels Ernestina is 'only too conventional' a choice as a wife: 'he began to feel sorry for himself—a brilliant man trapped, a Byron tamed'. His response to these tensions is thoroughly contradictory and symptomatic:

> After all, she was only a woman. There were so many things she must never understand: the richness of male life, the enormous difficulty of being one to whom the world was rather more than dress and home and children.
>
> All would be well when she was truly his; in his bed and in his bank... and of course in his heart, too. (*FLW*, p.114)

What this ironic note exposes are the paradoxes of male privilege which the individual Victorian male would have felt both beneficial and restrictive. Zoë Fairbairns reveals a similar situation in her recent historical novel *Stand We At Last*, in which Jonathan, a Victorian man of similar status to Charles, expresses a desperate sense of contradiction which finally drives him to suicide. Reflecting on his sister-in-law's judgements on his marriage he thinks

> Did she know how difficult it was for a man who must wait until middle age to marry? Did she guess how varied his tastes and adventures had been? And how difficult it had been to wean himself off them once he realised that his wife was going to provide no substitute for them in the physical aspect of marriage... he remembered the time he bought Helena a French night gown in the hope that she would turn into the sort of woman who wore such things. He had been in moral and physical turmoil in the first few years.[17]

These are the agonies of the powerful, trapped by their own exploitations. Charles's response to these tortuous conflicts is an idealising fantasy of a woman who challenges patriarchal restrictions and thus provides a possible escape from the problems, but who brings with her the corresponding anxiety of the challenge she poses to his own power. The very design of the novel, however, is to indulge this fantasy as it exposes it. The reason for this can be found in two related features of the book—its employment of a male narrator and the interconnected mystification of Sarah.

So far, we have tended to assume, as we did initially with Clegg and Urfe, that the character of Charles can be taken in some direct way as historically representative of masculinity. Of course this is not the case. Though the discussion of Charles as representative of Victorian masculinity has its place, he cannot be seen as an unmediated example. He is, after all, the fictional creation of a contemporary male author and, within the frame of the book, he is presented to us by a narrating voice which itself is not necessarily identifiable with the author in any direct way. Fowles made a very clear choice about his narrator. In an essay written whilst engaged on the first draft of the book, he writes of his preference for 'the ironic voice that the line of great nineteenth-century novelists, from Austen through to Conrad, all used so naturally',[18] a voice which elsewhere he describes as a 'narrating persona that is above all unpretentious and clubbable'.[19] As this suggests, the narrator is also a fictional character in his own right as Fowles makes plain in 'Notes on an unfinished novel':

> I have written myself another memorandum: You are not the 'I' who breaks into the illusion, but the 'I' who is part of it. In other words, the 'I' who will make first-person commentaries here and there in my story, and who will finally even enter it, will not be my real 'I' in 1967; but much more just another character, though in a different category from the purely fictional ones.[20]

The critic Peter Conradi suggests that 'this voice is the book's true hero',[21] a view which ought perhaps to be set beside the response of a feminist colleague that 'the narrator's a pig!'

The point we need to make is that the narrator's voice is distinctively and uncompromisingly a male one, with all the 'clubbability' that affords. What is more, he embodies glaring contradictions of his own. He is quite capable of calling frequent attention to the devastating effects of Victorian patriarchy on women, as when he calls the nineteenth century 'that black night of womanhood' (*FLW*, p.82), or when he applauds John Stuart Mill's 'brave attempt' at supporting women's suffrage which, he tells us, 'was greeted with smiles from the average man, guffaws from *Punch* (one joke showed a group of gentlemen besieging a female Cabinet minister, haw haw haw)' (*FLW*, p.101). In the first draft of the novel the narrator went so far as to deplore the treatment of women by men over the last hundred years and the miserably inadequate concessions made to equality, describing them as 'the grudging interest payments of a born welsher on his debts; the garish plastic beads that will distract the gullible natives' eyes from the real and continuing exploitation'.[22] Like the other passages mentioned, the sympathies of this hardly tally with the otherwise blatant male assumptions manifest elsewhere in the narrator's comments, notably with regard to the women of the novel. He displays a male camaraderie which extends to assessing at one point the various sexual appeals of the women characters:

> Of the three young women who pass through these pages Mary was, in my opinion, by far the prettiest. She had infinitely the most life, and infinitely the least selfishness; and physical charms to match. . . an exquisitely pure, if pink complexion, corn-coloured hair and delectably wide grey-blue eyes, eyes that invited male provocation and returned it as gaily as it was given. (*FLW*, p.68)

Later, commenting on Charles's sexual arousal whilst kissing Ernestina, the narrator says 'What Charles unconsciously felt was perhaps no more than the ageless attraction of shallow-minded women: that one may make of them what one wants.' (*FLW*, p.229) With an equally characteristic gesture, the narrator excuses the activities at Madame Terpsichore's with indulgent irony as 'this ancient and time-honoured form of entertainment' (*FLW*, p.264).

Of course the ironising function is crucial, but the premises are fundamentally masculine. The tone invokes a knowing male complicity between narrator and reader, which can be unfortunate if the reader is not male. It goes alongside the narrator's repeated nostalgia for the romance and mystery of the days when men were men and women were women. In chapter 17, he admits to being a 'heretic' in believing that there is too much communication between the sexes in the twentieth century. He envies the Victorians for their reserve which meant that 'Strangers were strange, and sometimes with an exciting, beautiful strangeness.' (*FLW*, p.115) By comparison with 'our own uninhibited, and unimaginative, age' (*FLW*, p.182), the supposedly repressed Victorians were 'quite as highly sexed as our own century' (*FLW*, p.232), and had 'a much keener, because less frequent, sexual pleasure than we do': they 'chose a convention of suppression, repression and silence to maintain the keenness of the pleasure', whereas we 'in destroying so much of the mystery, the difficulty, the aura of the forbidden, destroyed also a great deal of the pleasure' (*FLW*, p.234). He concludes that the 'gap between the sexes which so troubled Charles when Sarah tried to diminish it, certainly produced a greater force' (*FLW*, p.234). It is an odd viewpoint to reconcile with the earlier bewailing of this 'black night of womankind'. Such nostalgia only has real meaning as part of a contemporary male conception of sexual desire and pleasure such as Fowles himself defended to Sarah Benton as the 'mysterious quality in eroticism'.[23] Despite the intensity of feeling which overtakes Ernestina when Charles kisses her, the restrictions placed on female sexuality during the nineteenth century meant that most women would have experienced little pleasure from sexual contact, while the man would have been beset by paradoxical feelings of desire and guilt faced with the angelic status of his wife, to such an extent that in all probability he would have found sex with a prostitute less inhibiting and more pleasurable, as contemporary sources in fact recommended.[24] More than anything else, the narrator's nostalgia is a function of a contemporary male anxiety in the late 1960s.

The male complicity indicated here becomes highly ambiguous with regard to the way the narrator presents not simply Charles, but Sarah and her effect on Charles; and the ambiguities stem from Sarah's function in the book. She is the central term in the equation at the heart of Fowles's work, the mystery woman who is both a male fantasy and the catalyst for male redemption. In 'Notes on an unfinished novel' Fowles admits 'My two previous novels were both based on more or less disguised existential premises. I want this one to be no exception.' The Victorian age he sees as 'highly existentialist in many of its personal dilemmas', one of its similarities with his own time; and from his initial image of Sarah at the end of the Cobb he imagines 'an existentialist before his time, walks down the quay and sees that mysterious back, feminine, silent, also existentialist, turned to the horizon'.[25] In the book's terms, Sarah is 'the woman who was the door', while

Charles is 'the man without the key' (*FLW*, p.162).

For this reason, she is also posed as an insurgent against patriarchy's oppression of women, a self-inflicted martyr to its exploitations and finally outside the bounds of its law. In her challenge to convention Charles sees a potential for his own liberation through what she can seemingly offer him. This potential is not so much to do with Sarah herself as with his idealisation of her. At the same time that he begins to feel how conventional Ernestina is, he registers Sarah's attractions: 'It seemed clear to him that it was not Sarah in herself who attracted him—how could she, he was betrothed—but some emotion, some possibility she symbolized.' (*FLW*, p.114) The potential she reminds him of is his threatened freedom: later in the novel 'it was hardly Sarah he now thought of—she was merely the symbol around which had accreted all his lost possibilities, his extinct freedoms' (*FLW*, p.288). What this calls attention to is the process of male fantasy about women and, like Urfe, Charles is to be disintoxicated of his power through one of its central myths. When Grogan reprimands him over his treatment of Ernestina for having 'embroiled that innocent girl in your pursuit of self-knowledge' (*FLW*, p.340), the comment is apparently endorsed by the narrator at the end of the book when he remarks that 'life, however advantageously Sarah may in some ways seem to fit the role of Sphinx, is not a symbol, is not one riddle and one failure to guess it, is not to inhabit one face alone' (*FLW*, p.399). Put quite crudely, Charles has to grow up and relinquish the Oedipal desires which lead him to want to possess women by idealising them, an educative process which he assents to in his own lame verses:

What matter if the mother mocks

> The infant child's first feeble hands?
> What matter if today he fail
> Provided that at last he stands
> And breaks the blind maternal pale? (*FWL*, p.373)

The contradiction is, of course, that it is through his idealisation and attempts to appropriate Sarah that he is forced to a realisation of self and autonomy. It originates from her denial of his claims. As

93

a symbol of freedom for Charles Sarah is far from consolatory, challenging and rejecting as she does the need that obsesses him.

The point to bear in mind is not simply the way the narrating voice presents these ambiguities. There is also Fowles's position behind his surrogates. In her annotations to the original manuscripts, Elizabeth Fowles acutely commented on how evasive Fowles was about Sarah: 'The mystery of Sarah is not answered, wonder if it should be, but dislike what for me seems almost disintegration as if you really don't know when to—or how to explain her strangeness to youself.'[26] This insight indicates a process of both exorcism and indulgence of Sarah's mystery, the imaginative appeal of which Fowles himself explained directly to Melvyn Bragg in terms of his now familiar lost mother theme: 'its about what drives all of us who are novelists I think, that is the search for the lost relationship of the mother and the figure of Sarah at the end of the cobb is really the lost mother of infancy.' Later in the same interview in response to a question about Sarah's mysteriousness he has this to say:

> I did in the course of writing this book know I was dealing with this derivation of all art in my view, from the relationship between the infant and the vanished and un-noble mother. You know one can never get back. It's instant those months, a very early period of life when your identity showed with your mother. And therefore, in fact in very early drafts I described Sarah and gave her more details than appeared in the final thing. I realised she must be a mysterious woman because the figure in our unconscious is mysterious for all of us. And it's also partly because I think it is good that the reader has to add something.[27]

The effect of this is to make the book thoroughly ambiguous: it ostensibly charts Charles's escape from patriarchy's roles achieved through the impact on him of Sarah and her challenge to both his private life and his society; but in doing so it reinvokes the idealising male myth embodied in Sarah, presenting it for the indulgence of the reader. This is done by means of narrative strategies designed to make Sarah mysterious, one of which is the book's point of view.

L.R. Edwards is right when he says of Sarah that 'We never get to see inside her head', but that 'Far from being a weakness, this externality of character is itself part of the subject of [Fowles's] books', a subject which he takes to be partly 'masculine fantasies about the nature of the ideal woman'.[28] The corollary to this is Elizabeth Mansfield's view in her article on the original manuscripts of *The French Lieutenant's Woman* from which the comments by Elizabeth Fowles come. She stresses the manipulative effect of maintaining a mysteriousness about Sarah which Fowles's narrative tactics promote:

> From the first the author-narrator abnegated responsibility for answering the mystery of Sarah. . . The several portrayals of Sarah in the drafts indicate Fowles's unwillingness to explore possible definitions, but his final solution is the least transparent of the lot. What does not change, and what may finally determine the preservation of Sarah's mystery, is his use of point of view. He supports the position taken by the author-narrator in Chapter Thirteen and reports 'only the outward facts' about Sarah. We never know what she is thinking, only what she says and what the narration provides of Charles's interpretation. Thus, Sarah's mystery is maintained by narrative point of view.[29]

The deliberateness of this strategy on Fowles's part is indicated in his 'Notes on an unfinished novel' when, pondering what line of dialogue to give Sarah at the climax of a scene, he decides 'silence from her was better than any line she might have said'.[30] To see this at work in the book is to see the duplicity of Fowles's male imagination in action.

The access we have to Charles's mind and speculations is complemented by our having to guess at Sarah's through what Charles construes as the motives for her actions. Quite simply, we are given his construction of her and the narrative employs innumerable qualifying phrases which build her into an enigma. In her case it is always 'as if' or 'it seemed'. When Charles first sees her on the Cobb, he is 'intrigued' enough (*FLW*, p.12) to want to see her face. He addresses her for that purpose and 'She turned to look at him—or as it seemed to Charles, through him. . . Charles felt immediately as if he had trespassed. . . Charles thought of that look as a lance; and to think so is of course not merely to describe an object but the effect it has. He felt himself in that brief instant an unjust enemy; both pierced and deservedly diminished.'

(*FLW*, p.13) From the start, Charles registers Sarah as a challenge and as a reflection on his own power. What is more, the narrative indicates this process, warning us that his view of Sarah is an active reading of her in his own terms. The enigma of Sarah can, therefore, be seen as of Charles's making, existing within the boundaries of his male apprehension.

Equally important, however, is the way the narrating voice participates in this, showing Charles projecting an image onto Sarah and doing the same for the reader. The first view we have of her through the narrator presents her as 'like a living memorial to the drowned, a figure from myth' (*FLW*, p.9) and that elusiveness characterises the way the narrator describes her in general. When introducing her in chapters 4, 6 and 9, the narrator does so indirectly through other characters, avoiding any direct access to her psychology in any sustained way. We learn about her most directly in chapter 9, but it is still done in an oblique manner. We are told that Mrs Talbot associates Sarah with the 'starving heroines' of the 'more romantic literature' (*FLW*, p.49). Even when the narrator tells us, somewhat reluctantly, something direct about her, it is in such a way as to make her seem unusual and out of the ordinary. 'Sarah *was* intelligent', we are told, 'but her real intelligence belonged to a rare kind' (*FLW*, p.49): 'It was rather an uncanny... ability to classify other people's worth.' She saw people 'as they were and not as they tried to seem' because she had an 'instinctual profundity of insight' (*FLW*, p.50). She is thus given a position of superior judgement in an obscure way while at the same time the motives for her actions are deliberately shrouded in mystery by only giving us limited information: 'It would not be enough to say she was a fine moral judge of people. Her comprehension was broader than that, and if mere morality had been her touchstone she would not have behaved as she did—the simple fact of the matter being that she had not lodged with a female cousin at Weymouth' (*FLW*, p.50), with which the narrator changes the subject leaving the reader guessing as to where she *had* been in Weymouth. This tantalising excursion into her psychology and motives ends with a speculation about her marital status, present and future. We are told that she was 'too striking a girl' not to have suitors, but that her astute judgement meant she could see through them all too easily: 'Thus she appeared inescapably doomed to the one fate nature had so clearly spent many millions of years in evolving her to avoid: spinsterhood.' (*FLW*, p.51) With this suggestion that the most 'natural' destiny for a striking woman is marriage, the narrator again shifts the ground with the most overt example of the way other characters are used to present Sarah, Mrs Poulteney's list of 'fors and againsts on the subject of Sarah' (*FLW*, p.51), during which, while commenting on her apparent moral earnestness, he says: 'I cannot say what she might have been in our age; in a much earlier one I believe she would have been either a saint or an emperor's mistress. Not because of religiosity on the one hand, or sexuality on the other, but because of that fused rare power that was her essence—understanding and emotion.' (*FLW*, p.54).

It is the closest we get. Behind the apparent explaining, there is a process of mystification, attributing to Sarah a superior knowledge and an aura of mysteriousness, both of which lend Charles an undeserved reflected glory from her attentions to him. On the two prominent occasions when she is seen alone and not in relation to Charles, the narrator adopts a distance from the character which assumes a lack of omniscient knowledge that never occurs with his male character. At the end of chapter 12 after the confrontation with Mrs Poulteney, 'Sarah might be seen—though I cannot think by whom... standing at the open window of her unlit bedroom.' She is 'in her nightgown, with her hair loose' (*FLW*, p.83). She is alone with no one watching—except us: 'If you had gone closer still, you would have seen that her face was wet with silent tears.' (*FLW*, p.84) We are told that she was thinking of committing suicide; but we know she did not, not because we watch any longer but because 'We know she was alive a fortnight after this incident.' (*FLW*, p.84) It is a strangely evasive way to put this information and even more evasively the chapter ends with the narrator's provoking question 'Who is Sarah? Out of what shadows does she come?'

The answer is provided by the equally provoking opening to the next chapter: 'I do not know. This story I am telling is all imagination. These characters I create never existed outside my own mind... perhaps Charles is myself disguised. Perhaps it is only a game. Modern women like Sarah exist, and I have never understood them.' (*FLW*, p.85) This admission by the male narrator of his bewilderment at his own 'invention' is thoroughly paradoxical but easily explained. He has access to Charles's thoughts and even to Ernestina's—witness her 'sexual thought' in chapter 5 (*FLW*, p.30)—why not to Sarah's? Because the preservation of her mystery is essential to her function in the book. Indeed, it *is* her function in the book. Both the narrator and Charles serve as surrogates for this fantasy woven round the uncapturable mystique of the lost woman, an image designed to satisfy the demands of the male imagination. The role of the narrator is the one he invites the reader to adopt when looking up at Sarah in the window: 'Certainly I intended at this stage (*Chap. Thirteen—unfolding of Sarah's true state of mind*) to tell all—or all that matters. But I find myself suddenly like a man in the sharp spring night, watching from the lawn beneath that dim upper window.' (*FLW*, p.85) This is the novelist as peeping tom with the reader invited to play the voyeur.

It is a clever and effective piece of manipulation by Fowles which has the further function of structuring the theme of existential choice into the very design of the narrative; but it is a trick: as he told Melvyn Bragg with regard to this very passage, 'What I say on that subject [whether the author controls the characters] in *The French Lieutenant's Woman* is really a little bit of eye-wash. And I'm afraid I'm playing a sort of double trick on the reader. Of course I control the text [,] we all do.'[31] Part of the trick is the deliberate choice of narrative devices which create a complicity between male narrator, male character and a presumed male reader so that Sarah can be used to pander to male desires for an imagined encounter with the lost 'female' mystery which men project onto women. She is both outside the jurisdiction of the male narrator and, by virtue of that, fitted for the role of unattainable female. The only reality the narrator can imagine for Sarah is that she would not have delivered 'a chapter of revelation. She would instantly have turned, had she seen me there just as the old moon rose, and disappeared into the interior shadows.' (*FLW*, p.85) When, having listened to Sarah's confession about Varguennes, Charles suddenly gets a momentary glimpse of possible liberation from the sexual constraints of his time, 'a glimpse of an ideal world. . . a mythical world', that vision is significantly shadowed by 'a figure, a dark shadow, his dead sister [which] moved ahead of him, lightly, luringly, up the ashlar steps and into the broken columns' mystery' (*FLW*, pp.154-5). The mystery and shadow which Sarah comes from is, as Gilbert Rose speculates in his marvellously evocative piece on the book, maternal.[32] Charles embodies the male deprived of his mother, who died giving birth to his stillborn sister (*FLW*, p.16), caught in a material world in which 'there is no mystery. No romance' (*FLW*, p.14), and searching for consolation. Sarah is made the enigma of his Oedipal quest and his story invites the indulgence of the reader's own fantasies.

All this, as one might expect, puts 'Sarah' well and truly within the bounds of the male sexual imagination and the effect of that on some male readers can be measured by Wolfe's response to what he calls the 'fertility' of Sarah's mystery. For him, it accounts 'for much of the novel's spell': 'Women need to exude secrecy and mystery; men need to penetrate this female magic. The necessary collision of these two drives can be fatal.'[33] This comment is made without any apparent critical perspective and it exemplifies the potential function of male-defined art which Fraser Harrison has identified. In his pertinent remarks on John Berger's analysis of the genre of paintings of the nude, Harrison suggests that the female nude as painted by men involves a deliberate artistic selection of images of women at a point of potential submission, for the purpose of 'depriving the woman of her sexual autonomy'. Berger himself sees paintings of female nudes as 'offering up their femininity to be displayed' and Harrison expands this by saying that the female subject 'can only surrender to the invading gaze of the male spectator, she is defenceless. She is, however, seen to be gladly surrendering: she happily, though modestly, accepts his inspection.' Harrison pinpoints how male-orientated art can service the male imagination and, significantly, male power: 'Female defencelessness is precious to the male's sexual vanity; his belief in his own potency is enhanced by the sight of a woman who has been denied the means of resistance. The artist who implies that there is an alliance between the woman's body and the desire of the male onlooker which the woman herself is powerless to restrain is furnishing a deeply reassuring image.'[34]

In the case of narrative art, the dynamic of the form makes this relationship between artist, object and audience complex in other ways, of course, which necessitates adapting Harrison's suggestions; but their general drift typifies the function of the narrative viewpoint which characterises *The French Lieutenant's Woman*. Sarah is, equally, not as defenceless as the nudes Harrison describes, but this serves merely to compound the situation in the book. For she is presented as a dangerous woman, a *femme fatale* whose mystery derives in part from her status as social outcast and threat to the patriarchal order; and having been posed in this way, she *is* won and by force. Her dangerous quality is patently there as a spice to gratify a male viewpoint, an imagined dalliance with danger whose complications are instructive for our purposes.

In Charles's mind, the significantly heart-shaped echinoderms or 'tests' from the Undercliff become linked with thoughts 'of women lying asleep on sunlit ledges' (*FLW*, p.119), and increasingly his involvement with Sarah develops a sexual aura around her. The link between her and the primitive Undercliff allows them both to act as correlatives for Charles's own repressed sexuality. When Charles drives through the gates of Winsyatt into 'his inheritance', the 'absurd adventure in the Undercliff was forgotten. Immense duties, the preservation of this peace and order, lay ahead, as they had lain ahead of so many young men of his family in the past. Duty—that was his real wife, his Ernestina and his Sarah'. (*FLW*, p.171) It is to this patriarchal order and Charles's final entry into it that Sarah, 'a woman most patently dangerous' (*FLW*, p.128), poses such a threat, and it is manifest in two ways.

Firstly she echoes the sexually desirable women of Charles's past, disturbing in Charles recollections of 'his time in Paris' (*FLW*, p.64) on a number of occasions. What he sees as 'the suppressed sensuality of her mouth' and her dark eyes are associated for him with 'foreign women—to be frank (much franker than he would have been to himself) with foreign beds. This marked a new stage of his awareness of Sarah. He had realized she was more intelligent and independent than she seemed; he now guessed darker qualities.' (*FLW*, p.105) She reminds him of another fictional *femme fatale*: 'as he looked down at the face beside him, it was suddenly, out of nowhere, that Emma Bovary's name sprang into his mind. Such allusions are comprehensions; and temptations.' (*FLW*, p.106) In the Assembly Rooms during the concert, 'his mind wandered back to Sarah, to visual images, attempts to recall that face, that mouth, that generous mouth. Undoubtedly it awoke some memory in him, too tenuous, perhaps too general, to trace to any source in his past; but it unsettled him and haunted him, by calling to some hidden self he hardly knew existed.' (*FLW*, p.114) The sexuality ascribed to Sarah is underlined by the narrator's attribution to her on a number of occasions of 'a kind of wildness' (*FLW*, p.121). In fact the narrator continually suggests her sexuality, usually in an oblique manner which carries a promise of availability. When Charles and Sarah are surprised by Sam and Mary, Sarah's smile to Charles is described as 'something as strange, as shocking, as if she had thrown off her clothes' (*FLW*, p.161). Her look has 'an anger, a defiance; as if she were naked before him, yet proud to be so' (*FLW*, p.152). Such hints anticipate what is the central dynamic of Charles's quest for Sarah—his sexual conquest of her later in the book.

The other element in her dangerousness is linked with this implied sexuality—her status as both fallen woman and 'new woman'. Sarah stands outside the middle-class norms of her age by her breaking of taboos in a way which 'seemed almost to assume some sort of equality of intellect with him' (*FLW*, p.124). This 'presumption of intellectual equality Charles sees as 'a suspect resentment against man' (*FLW*, p.159) which manifests itself in her account of her betrayal by Varguennes. The vicar tells Mrs Poulteney that Sarah suffers from a 'fixed delusion that the lieutenant is an honourable man' (*FLW*, p.35) and 'honourable man' is a phrase which reverberates through the book, implicitly questioning whether there can be such a phenomenon or whether it is a contradiction in terms. What we learn from Sarah is that her self-martyrdom as an outcast woman is designed as an indictment of men in general. They are, as her first look makes Charles feel, 'an unjust enemy' (*FLW*, p.13). She appears quite specifically as the representative of all women exploited and oppressed by male society, a defiant embodiment of its injustices and thereby outside its control: 'there are not spirits generous enough to understand what I have suffered and why I suffer... I feel cast on a desert island, imprisoned, condemned, and I know not what crime it is for.' (*FLW*, p.124) When she first met Varguennes, she did not know 'that men can be both very brave and very false... He seemed a gentleman' (*FLW*, p.147); but he was 'a man without scruples, a man of caprice, of a passionate selfishness' (*FLW*, p.152). She tells Charles that she sees him as different from the rest of society—i.e. other men—: 'You are not cruel, I know you are not cruel' (*FLW*, p.125), but in one sense this is the key to the self-deception practised by Charles. After hearing the outcome of her story his response is 'But my dear Miss Woodruff, if every woman who'd been deceived by some unscrupulous member of my sex were to behave as you have—I fear the country would be full of outcasts', to which she replies 'It is.' (*FLW*, p.157) Charles's assumption that he is different is refuted by his own betrayal of Ernestina which reproduces in essence Varguennes's relations with Sarah: Ernestina tells him 'you are a monster', to which he replies 'You will meet other men... not broken by life. Honourable men, who will...' (*FLW*, p.329). It is Charles's complicity along with all other men in the social exploitation of women that we can see indicated in his response while Sarah tells her story of Varguennes's supposed betrayal: 'He saw the scene she had not detailed: her giving herself. He was at one and the same time Varguennes enjoying her and the man who sprang forward and struck him down; just as Sarah was to him both an innocent victim and a wild, abandoned woman.' (*FLW*, pp.153-4) The book itself reproduces this paradox by revealing the process of male power, as it does here, whilst at the same time casting Sarah as the mythical mysterious woman.

Part of this ambiguity comes through the suggestion that what Sarah practises on Charles is a justifiable revenge on men. What Charles later comes to understand as 'her feeling of resentment, of an unfair because remediable bias in society' (*FLW*, p.351) is represented in hints throughout the book, as when speaking of her sense of injustice Sarah says 'when I read of the Unionists' wild acts of revenge, part of me understands. Almost envies them, for they know where and how to wreak their revenge. And I am powerless.' (*FLW*, p.149) When Sarah reveals to Charles, in so far as she ever does, the reasons for her deceptions, she explains 'There is one thing in which I have not deceived you. I loved you... I think from the moment I saw you. In that, you were never deceived. What duped you was my loneliness. A resentment, an envy, I don't know. I don't know.' (*FLW*, p.308) Charles feels himself to have been 'no more than the dupe of your imaginings' (*FLW*, p.309), though it would be more accurate to say he was the dupe of his own preconceptions.

Yet while Sarah's status as social outcast, emergent feminist and revenging *femme fatale* displays an awareness in the book of the patriarchal oppression of women, the role is equally an imaginative exploitation of her as a tantalising woman of mystery and a fantasy substitute for the mother figure. In this respect, Charles's thoughts after nearly being discovered with Sarah by Sam could equally be applied to the function of the book for Fowles and the male reader: 'all variations on that agelessly popular male theme: "You've been playing with fire, my boy."' (*FLW*, p.164) The rationale for casting her in this way is itself part of the *femme fatale* tradition, in which, according to sex historian Reay Tannahill, women 'dominated and even, like the praying mantis, killed the men they loved or coveted. And the men quite enjoyed it. Until the nineteenth century, there had been no precise stereotype of the predatory feminist... but the Victorians' muddled blend of public courtliness and private guilt made it necessary to create one.'[35] As with all such fantasies, in which men are what Swinburne called 'the powerless victim[s] of the furious rage of a beautiful woman',[36] there is a devious male satisfaction to be gained from the masochism involved. Tannahill reflects how 'Times change. Whereas the arrogant imaginary woman acted as a sexual stimulant to the Victorian male, the flesh-and-blood feminist today often alarms her lover into impotence.'[37] Though Sarah is not a stereotypical example, Fowles's book is quite overtly a fantasy of dominance and submission in which she is made both sexual and threatening. The present-day sense of male guilt and anxiety comes through strongly in two crucial areas of the book—Charles's visits to the arch-misogynist Dr Grogan, and the sexual encounter between Charles and Sarah.

It is Grogan who occupies chapter 19, separating the two meetings between Charles and Sarah during which she confesses about Varguennes, and as such he plays a key role in generating suspicion about Sarah's motivation. Grogan inhabits the 'masculine, more serious world' (*FLW*, p.132) of the confirmed bachelor. He classifies Sarah as suffering from a form of hysterical melancholy and warns Charles 'You must not think she is like us men, able to reason clearly'. (*FLW*, p.137) At this point in the chapter, Fowles intercuts a scene in which we see Sarah in bed with Millie, Mrs Poulteney's maid. The treatment of this episode is intriguing. It has a dual function: it ironises the assumption of male superiority just expressed by Grogan and at the same time it treats the implications of the two girls sleeping together in an ambiguous and suggestive manner. Sarah's sleeping with Millie is finally explained as a concerned tenderness for the younger girl, but at first it is tantalisingly suggested as a potential lesbian encounter which might explain Sarah's mystery—'A thought has swept into your mind.' (*FLW*, p.137) We are, in fact, reassured that 'some vices were then so unnatural that they did not exist' (*FLW*, p.137) and the point seems thus to be an ironic comment on Victorian sexual mores. Yet this is far from the final impression of the episode. The narrator ends his comments on it by saying that no doubt somewhere 'a truly orgastic lesbianism existed then; but we may ascribe this very common Victorian phenomenon of women sleeping together far more to the desolating arrogance of contemporary man than to a more suspect motive. Besides, in such wells of loneliness is not any coming together closer to humanity than perversity?' (*FLW*, p.139) While the nod in the direction of Radcliffe Hall's novel suggests a deference towards lesbianism, the censorious note of 'suspect' and 'perversity' suggest the opposite; and it is thus we are returned from 'these two innocents... to that other more rational, more learned and altogether more nobly gendered pair', the 'two lords of creation' who are discussing Sarah with their own blatant male presumptions. The issue of lesbianism, the ultimate female autonomy, recurs at the end of the book when Charles visits Sarah in the Rossetti house (*FLW*, p.389), while the anxiety occasioned by such fear of women is reproduced when Charles goes back to see Grogan later in the book and the true dimensions of the doctor's misogyny are revealed. Grogan reads Sarah's behaviour as part of a general female inclination 'to lure mankind into their power' (*FLW*, p.193). Speaking as if he had himself personal experience of men becoming victims of dangerous women, he voices what he sees as their motivations: 'I am cast out. But I shall be revenged.' (*FLW*, p.194) Under Grogan's influence, Charles admits to feeling 'like a man possessed against his will' (*FLW*, p.196) and ready to do 'Anything to be rid of her—without harm to her' (*FLW*, p.197) including sending Sarah to a 'model' asylum. To cement this purgation, Grogan lends Charles the La Roncière trial account, one of the vast number of Victorian misogynistical tracts. Charles's initial reaction is shock: 'he had no idea that such perversions existed—and in the pure and sacred sex' (*FLW*, p.204). He feels a total loss of respect for women: 'Behind the most innocent faces lurked the vilest iniquities. He was Sir Galahad shown Guinevere to be a whore' (*FLW*, p.205), despite which the recollection of 'Those eyes' (*FLW*, p.206) sends him off to meet Sarah at the barn.

The misogyny theme has a twofold importance. It exposes the fear of women and sexuality as the psychological breeding ground for the schizophrenic male response. At the same time it lays the ground for the quite contradictory effect of the sexual climax of the book. That climax in the Endicott Family Hotel is the hidden dynamic for the obsession with Sarah and its effective function is intensified by the factors outlined so far, the 'endlessly repeated luring-denying... the cock-tease' as Fowles has called it.[38] The visit to Madame Terpsichore's, the encounter with Sarah the prostitute, the spurious false ending in which Charles fantasises that he has done 'the moral, the decent, the correct thing' (*FLW*, p.288) and married Ernestina, are all tactics to delay the gratification further. The actual encounter itself enacts the same pattern, but adding the central ingredient, imagined sexual congress.

The first point to notice about this sequence is the play made between our knowledge that Sarah has manipulated the situation, and the role she enacts for Charles of the submissive woman. Her control of the encounter maintains her autonomous status, an important element in her fantasy function. She sends Charles the address; she pretends to have a sprained ankle, planning in advance by buying the bandage as a strategy presumably to get him alone in her room without social inhibitions (*FLW*, p.242); and she reveals that she has lied about Varguennes, being still a virgin. But before any of this becomes apparent at least during a first reading, Charles as the stand-in for the author-reader has enacted a forceful physical possession of Sarah little short of rape. The other factor to consider contradicts this physical dominance entirely—Charles's premature ejaculation.

The submissive role Sarah adopts is significant since, though it is a trick to draw Charles on, it puts her in a position of apparent vulnerability displayed nowhere else in the book: 'as if all her mystery, this most intimate self, was exposed before him: proud and submissive, bound and unbound, his slave and his equal' (*FLW*, p.301). Charles's 'violent sexual desire' (*FLW*, p.302), though it is seen as specifically his response imposed upon her, acts as an urgent imperative for the culmination of the fantasy woven round Sarah: his 'terrible need' for her is 'to possess her, to melt into her, to burn, to burn, to burn to ashes on that body and in those eyes.' (*FLW*, p.302). Charles's presumptions about Sarah proliferate in marked abundance as his desire grows more frantic: '*as if* by an instinctive gesture, yet one she half dared to calculate, her hand reached shyly out'; '*as if* she knew she was hurting him'; 'this was a face that *seemed* almost self-surprised, as lost as himself'; 'She turned her head away... almost *as if* he repelled her; but her bosom *seemed* to arch imperceptibly [*sic*] towards him'; 'She *seemed* to half step, half fall towards him.' (*FLW*, p.303—my emphasis) At the same time, there is an insistence on Charles's quite brutal physical dominance over Sarah: 'Their mouths met with a wild violence that shocked both; made her avert her lips.' (*FLW*, p.303) 'He swept her up and carried her through to the bedroom. She lay where he threw her across the bed, half-swooned, one arm flung back.' 'With a frantic brutality, as he felt his ejaculation about to burst, he found the place and thrust. Her body flinched again, as it had when her foot fell from the stool. He conquered that instinctive constriction'. (*FLW*, p.304)

In its structure, this passage duplicates the insistent urgency, violence and brevity of male sexuality in its 'orthodox' form. It creates a tension between imagined sexual possession of Sarah, and all she stands for, and the anxiety of male desire itself; and this tension is at the root of the effect achieved by the ending of the book. Charles's hasty climax, his corresponding disregard for Sarah's sexual response and his ensuing guilt seem both absurdly inadequate and quite appropriate as manifestations of his 'love' for Sarah. Effectively, he has merely used her to fulfil his desire as part of the more general presumption by men that male sexual pleasure *is* sexual pleasure. His momentary abandonment to desire is shown to be totally within the jurisdiction of the patriarchal order he himself embodies: he hears footsteps outside and his immediate response is 'A police officer, perhaps. The Law.' (*FLW*, p.305) He tells her he is worse than Varguennes: 'Her only answer was to press his hand, as if to deny and hush him. But he was a man. "What is to become of us?"' (*FLW*, p.305) Charles is blatantly caught in the contradictions of masculinity in his paradoxical reaction to Sarah's unconventional behaviour. When she seems ready to accept responsibility for what has happened 'Charles was flooded with contempt for his sex: their triviality, their credulity, their selfishness. But he was of that sex, and there came to him some of its old devious cowardice: Could not this perhaps be no more than his last fling, the sowing of the last wild oats?' (*FLW*, p.306) But with the revelation of Sarah's duplicity Charles's reaction is an abrupt about-turn:

> She had not given herself to Varguennes. She had lied. All her conduct, all her motives in Lyme Regis had been based on a lie. But for what purpose. Why? Why? Why?
> Blackmail!
> To put him totally in her power!
> And all those loathsome succubi of the male mind, their fat fears of a great feminine conspiracy to suck the virility from their veins, to prey upon their idealism, melt them into wax and mould them to their evil fancies... these, and a surging back to credibility of the hideous evidence adduced in the La Roncière appeal, filled Charles's mind with an apocalyptic horror. (*FLW*, pp.307-8)

What this sequence shows is Charles struggling to come to terms with a woman who is outside the parameters of his control and thus must pose a threat to his power. The effect of this is capped as Sarah 'castrated the accusations in his mind' (*FLW*, p.308) by admitting the deception and asserting that she did love him but 'There can be no happiness for you with me. You cannot marry me, Mr Smithson.' (*FLW*, p.309) The paradox Charles has to face in Sarah and which goes some way towards explaining the present-day relevance of the book, is that she represents an ethic which acts both as an indictment of male power and a potential liberation from it. When Charles asks her how she can tell him to go after their sexual union, her response is 'Why not, if I love you?' (*FLW*, p.306) Sarah offers a freedom from patriarchal restraint which is also a denial of the necessary relation between the sexes which is one of its founding mythologies. After the event, Charles can see only the reinstitution of patriarchal roles through marriage to Sarah, or at least a fixed relationship: in his letter of decision he writes 'I am resolved, my sweet and mysterious Sarah, that what now binds us shall bind us for evermore.' (*FLW*, p.320) Sarah, on the other hand, offers the uncomfortable uncertainty and challenge of self-determination, choice and a defiance of patriarchal models.

Yet whilst she undoubtedly embodies this ethic of freedom and the indictment of patriarchy, Sarah is *used* both to teach men a lesson about themselves and as an instrument for imaginary gratification. The subsequent denial of a continuing relationship between her and Charles merely serves to heighten the potential for what Fowles, we may remember, calls 'the characteristic male preoccupation with loss, non-fulfilment, non-consummation'.[39] It is essential in terms of Fowles's sexual imagination: the quest is now repeated but under the new conditions of Charles's enforced and precarious sense of 'freedom', in which the oppressor becomes 'the outcast, the not like other men': 'When he had had his great vision of himself freed from his age, his ancestry and class and country, he had not realized how much the freedom was embodied in Sarah; in the assumption of a shared exile.' (*FLW*, p.366) His exile is the emblem of the male exile from the mother figure and all it implies for Fowles in terms of values and redemption.

The mythical status of that redemption when articulated in these terms is demonstrated by the way Fowles chose to deal with the ending of the book. In the 'Hardy and the Hag' essay he quotes the double ending as an example of the male imagination's insistent 'need to embark upon further stories. . . to search for an irrecoverable experience':

> I wrote and printed two endings to *The French Lieutenant's Woman* because from early in the first draft I was torn intolerably between wishing to reward the male protagonist (my surrogate) with the woman he loved and wishing to deprive him of her—that is, I wanted to pander to both the adult and the child in myself. I had experienced a very similar predicament in my two previous novels. Yet I am now very clear that I am happier, where I gave two, with the unhappy ending, and not in any way for objective critical reasons, but simply because it has seemed more fertile and onward to my whole being as a writer.[40]

In one sense what Fowles is saying is that the denial of fulfilment in imaginative terms serves, as with Hardy, to stimulate his imagination to undertake another quest, write another fiction. At the same time it is possible to read in this and in the unhappy ending of the book itself an implicit injunction that no good can come from the continuing desire to pander to the Oedipal trauma; that change can only be brought about by men effectively taking responsibility for changing themselves rather than looking towards a mythical solution from women, a solution which is both the creation and mark of male power. The final sense of *The French Lieutenant's Woman* is much more about being liberated *from* Sarah, the mythical shadow haunting male experience and nurturing its desire for power, than being liberated *by* her. This dilemma, and the troubling anxiety which accompanies it, is manifest in Charles's increasingly contradictory attitude to his quest and its object: 'he became increasingly unsure of the frontier between the real Sarah and the Sarah he had created in so many such dreams: the one Eve personified, all mystery and love and profundity, and the other a half-scheming, half-crazed governess from an obscure seaside town.' (*FLW*, p.367) As yet, Charles is incapable of stepping outside his own male thinking, though he has made a partial break with his society: Sarah remains his creation, whether as ideal or *femme fatale*, and he cannot see any third possibility outside the limits of this enclosed paradox. His love of Tennyson's poem *Maud*, itself an incisive portrayal of male fantasy in action, suggests that he identifies with the bereft hero rather than seeing his own tendencies mirrored in that character's incurable and destructive idealisation. While Fowles can quote appropriately from that poem as an epigram—'ah for a man to arise in me, That the man I am may cease to be!' (*FLW*, p.295)—Charles shows little capacity for meeting the challenge for his species to adapt to the new conditions signified by the emergence of women like Sarah. What both forms of the ending insist on is the very slight possibility of this happening easily.

In the shared run-up to the two endings, Charles is shown still desiring to act out the mythical roles of his patriarchal outlook and being frustrated in the task: 'He had come to raise her from penury, from some crabbed post in a crabbed house. In full armour, ready to slay the dragon—and now the damsel had broken all the rules.' (*FLW*, p.381) Finding Sarah a free, working woman, he is again bewildered by her desire for autonomy: 'I do not want to share my life', she tells him, 'I wish to be what I am, not what a husband, however kind, however indulgent, must expect me to become in marriage.' (*FLW*, p.385) Her 'new self-knowledge and self-possession' (*FLW*, p.386) provoke Charles, going quite contrary to his own Darwinism, into saying 'you cannot reject the purpose for which woman was brought into creation', what he calls 'the natural law', whilst in the same breath asserting 'I too have changed. I have learnt much of myself, of what was previously false in me.' (*FLW*, p. 386) Sarah's answer, with its suggestion that male 'love' inevitably involves possession, and his response sound a note of threat to male prestige that goes to the heart of the book:

'It is not you I fear. It is your love for me. I know only to well that nothing remains sacrosanct there.'
...perhaps he did at last begin to grasp her mystery. Some terrible perversion of human sexual destiny had begun: he was no more than a footsoldier, a pawn in a far vaster battle; and like all battles it was not about love, but about possession and territory. (*FLW*, p.387)

The emerging autonomy of women and the challenge it presents to male power, which Charles and/or the narrator sees as a 'terrible perversion of sexual destiny', demand an evolutionary adaptation which Charles finds impossible. It demands a change in his outlook and an accompanying abdication of power which he cannot accommodate since his thinking is still framed in terms of the necessary relation of the sexes subserving a dominantly male idea, a mythical resolution.

The first ending gives Charles such a resolution. In it, he meets his daughter and this, as Gilbert Rose demonstrates, links up the whole pattern of the lost female and the bereft child which is woven through the book like a hidden consolation or a distraction from the frustrations of reality: 'Like the French Lieutenant's Woman's daughter, or the daughter of that other Sarah, the novelist is the child of one parent only. Aroused from sleep or taken from his nurse's arms, with fear and curiosity, wishing both to return and to explore, he comes to sit upon the knee of the stranger who dangles a watch.'[41] Against that, there is Sarah observing Charles with 'a curiosity: a watching for the result of an experiment' (*FLW*, p.389). When he asks 'Shall I ever understand your parables?' she shakes her head 'with a mute vehemence', the form of his question indicating how correct her answer is. The Charles of this ending is both apparently open to learn and the continuing victim-perpetrator of his sex's mythologies. When he told his lawyer Montague that he had to see Sarah because 'she continues to haunt me', Montague evades comment by saying 'You must question the Sphinx', a fatalistic resignation to Charles's obstinate pursuit of his destiny, to which he adds 'As long as you bear in mind what happened to those who failed to solve the enigma.' (*FLW*, p.376) At least Charles is deflected from his self-regarding presumptions by having to amuse his daughter (*FLW*, p.393), though it would be too much to see this as suggesting Fowles foresaw the political need for men to take on the responsibility and values of childcare.

In the second ending, Charles's misogynistical misconceptions about Sarah win the day—'she had manipulated him. She would do so to the end'—and he leaves abruptly. He feels, in an echo planted earlier in the book, like 'the last honourable man on the way to the scaffold' (*FLW*, p.397), and we are left with the image of him pacing down the deserted embankment, 'a man behind the invisible gun-carriage on which rests his own corpse' (*FLW*, p.399), the only mourner at the imaginary funeral of his kind. Intriguingly, the narrator's position becomes increasingly overt in its endorsement of Sarah in this final version. We are invited to see Charles's leaving Sarah in such a way as his 'final foolishness', and Sarah's 'battle for territory' as 'a legitimate uprising of the invaded against the perennial invader' (*FLW*, p.398). For his philosophical conclusion on life, the narrator adapts Marx's definition of it as '*the actions of men* (and of women) *in pursuit of their ends*' and adds 'The fundamental principle that should guide these actions, that I believe myself always guided Sarah's, I have set as the second epigraph.' (*FLW*, p.398) The epigraph is Arnold's—'True piety is *acting what one knows.*' (*FLW*, p.394) And despite his despairing pose, the disintoxicated Charles, who we can presume had until now only acted what he imagined, 'has at last found an atom of faith in himself, a true uniqueness, on which to build' by realising that Sarah is not the Sphinx, its question or its answer.

This ambiguous and muted hope for the future is symptomatic of the effect of *The French Lieutenant's Woman* as a whole. It remains a book which, while it raises the whole problem of the way men see and appropriate women, also purveys an integrally 'romantic' appeal which reproduces that problem. This paradox was latent in Fowles's original conception of the central situation. In the 'Notes on an unfinished novel' he records the genesis of the book in terms of 'a visual image. A woman stands at the end of a deserted quay and stares out to sea.' In its effect he felt the image had 'some sort of imminent power. It was obviously mysterious. It was vaguely romantic.' He remembers registering the woman as 'An outcast. I didn't know her crime, but I wished to protect her. That is, I began to fall in love with her. Or her stance. I didn't know which.'[42] The male protectiveness and idealisation became both the impulse and the subject of the book, a fact which Fowles came to realise only after the event as a personal exorcism of his obsessive concern for the female archetype. To Melvyn Bragg he said

112

I've never really known what I was doing until I wrote *The French Lieutenant's Woman*. And even now I can still see things in it which I didn't realise at the time. I think the fact that freedom plays a considerable part in the novel is because I was trying to get free or to make objective this sort of relationship we all have with the vanished mother of infancy. In other words, I was psycho-analysing myself if you like. I didn't realise that when I was writing the book.[43]

This act of bringing this myth into consciousness, of freeing himself by writing it out, is one which allowed for a definite advance in his next novel, *Daniel Martin*. In that book he attempts the ambitious task of stepping outside his own activity not simply as a male, but as a male novelist. In doing so, he gives his most overtly political analysis of the action of male power in the contemporary world and shows at the same time that the exorcism is far from complete.

5

Escaping the script — the politics of change: *Daniel Martin*

In his reassessment of contemporary Marxism, *Farewell to the Working Class*, André Gorz presents a view from the male Left of the redemptive role of feminism which has much in common with Fowles: 'post-industrial socialism—that is communism—will be female or will not exist at all', Gorz argues, adding 'This implies a cultural revolution which will eliminate the principle of performance, the ethic of competition, accumulation and the rat-race at the level of both individual behaviour and social relations, replacing them with the supremacy of the values of reciprocity, tenderness, spontaneity and love of life in all its forms.'[1] *Daniel Martin* presents Fowles's critique of consumer capitalism and its ills, and like Gorz he sees political and personal redemption from this society, for men as well as for women, in terms of 'female' values transposed into a form of communism. In doing so he raises again what is arguably the single most critical issue posed by the contemporary women's movement along with the associated one of nuclear disarmament—the relation of men to the values contained in feminism and the accompanying politics of change. We have seen this issue as central to his books in a number of ways and, in terms of the male responses they typify, as contradictory. In this he is symptomatic. As Gorz's views indicate, men on the Left are increasingly drawn, not to say argued, into a realisation that, in its values and practice, feminist politics embodies *the* major progressive force in the contemporary West. Gorz believes that feminism's aim now should be 'to win over men both inside and outside the home to subvert the traditional sexual division of labour; and to abolish not only the hegemony of the values of virility but these values themselves, both in relations between the sexes and society at large.'[2]

The danger in men seeing women as offering salvation lies in a male appropriation of feminism for their own ends rather than changing in response to its challenge, and we have seen this also displayed in Fowles's novels. Two critical questions remain—whether by espousing the values of feminism men are in some way necessarily containing or defusing them; and in what ways men *are* to abdicate from the social legacy of patriarchal power. Gorz puts this in terms of a dialectic of change 'at the level of both individual behaviour and social relations'.[3] *Daniel Martin* shows such a process at work and the contradictions involved. It is Fowles at his most politically overt, committed to the view that men must and can change; yet the traces of the male mythologies, which he tries every possible narrative strategy to objectify, linger deviously.

Such a paradox is almost inescapable given Fowles's view of the impact of feminism on men. Sarah Benton asked him if feminism had taught him anything new about men:

> Yes, he says, it affected his writing of *Daniel Martin* in particular. He thinks it has affected most men writers today, but perhaps only because they fear hostility to their male chauvinism. So what is it that men feel about themselves, the power they exercise as their birthright in the world? 'Guilt. Men have been carrying this terrible load for thousands of years, this great superstructure.[4]

It is a disappointing answer by comparison with the work the novel itself does in exposing and demystifying male power, but then the novel itself is far from exempt from contradictions.

The evidence for the effect of feminism is built into the scheme of *Daniel Martin*. Its central male character is presented as the perpetrator-victim of the male capitalist ethic, while Jane, the left-wing Communist Party sympathiser, acts as his redeemer, in his eyes at least. Noticeably, though Jane is touched by the women's movement through her daughter Ros, Fowles does not make her a feminist *per se*, preferring to have her voice the values of a humanistic communism in her indictment of the self-seeking world which Dan inhabits. As he comes increasingly to feel that Jane offers a redemptive solution to his life and that his 'political indifference and ignorance needed reprimand' (*DM*, p.419), so the narrative reveals Dan idealising and desperately trying to appropriate her. Fowles's undoubted awareness of this process is written into the novel's structure, which presents the book as ostensibly the production of Daniel Martin himself as novel writer.

Dan's 'novel' is both his personal rediscovery and the emblem of his new-found social commitment under Jane's influence, his voluntary abdication from the world of power and illusion epitomised by the cinema. *Fowles's* novel, on the other hand, shows Daniel's to be a continuation of the male fictions he has tried to escape. What Fowles attempts is to show up the obsessive mythologising of the male novelist, his own condition, in action. It is a remarkably ambitious and inescapably impossible task, suitably so perhaps if, as he admits, the generative impulse of the book was guilt. What is positive about his project is its very attempt at awareness. It is Fowles's version as a male writer of Gramsci's 'philosophy of praxis' as signalled in the book itself: '*The philosophy of praxis is consciousness full of contradictions, in which the philosopher himself, understood both individually and as an entire social group, not merely grasps the contradictions, but posits himself as an element of the contradiction and elevates this element to a principle of knowledge and therefore of action.*' (*DM*, p.210) The chinese-box effect of the book derives from Fowles's attempt finally to objectify his own obsessional fantasies of the lost woman by writing about Daniel writing about them. As a result, we need to consider the narrative strategies of the book and how they shape these issues. First, though, we should establish how centrally *Daniel Martin* concerns itself with the contemporary male condition, one that is not limited to the individual character.

Daniel is the emblem of his generation's failures, 'no more than an extreme example of the general case' (*DM*, p.94), just as his cinema world is the emblem of western society's wider failures. He and his self-disgust are representative of a post-war malaise which the book locates as a specifically male condition. The crisis inheres in the role of the professional career-orientated male within advanced capitalist society and the novel's view shares a great deal with writers like Andrew Tolson who see this as a crisis of masculinity:[5] 'So many other students he had known at Oxford had been sucked down into this world, with all its illusions of instant power; were in politics now, in television, on Fleet Street; had become cogs in the communication machine, stifled all ancient conviction for the sake of career, some press-lord's salary.' (*DM*, p.277) Inevitably, the contemporaries Daniel has in mind are men. There are a number of points in the book where Daniel puts forward this sense of a betrayal of integrity for the sake of power or success, of men selling out to the illusory values of media power, none of them more pointed than when he meets Barney Dillon on the plane back from Hollywood:

> I certainly could not call Barney a failure in worldly terms; yet something of that also hung about him—indeed has continued to hang around all my Oxford generation. As with Ken Tynan, so many others, I certainly can't except myself, destiny then pointed to far higher places than the ones actually achieved. Perhaps we were too self-conscious, too aware of one another and what was expected of us, too scared of seeming pretentious; and then, in the 1950s, we were fatally undercut and isolated by the whole working-class, anti-university shift in the English theatre and the novel. Tynan's famous rave for *Look Back in Anger* was also a kind of epitaph over *our* hopes and ambitions—over the framework of middle-class tradition and culture that we had all been willy-nilly confined in. All this reduced us to watching and bitching; to satire; to climbing on whatever cultural or professional bandwagon came to hand, accepting the fool's gold of instant success. That is why so many became journalists, critics, media men, producers and directors; grew so scared of their pasts and their social class, and never recovered. (*DM*, p.109)

The Le Carré-like defeatism here is both expressed and critically probed through Dan's overview of himself and, as we shall see, Fowles's detachment from his character. It is a book which, like the prototype Fowles had in mind whilst writing it, Flaubert's *A Sentimental Education*, is designed to act 'as a cultural history of its time', according to interviewer Mel Gussow.[6]

Barney Dillon, like Dan, exemplifies the stultifying effects of easy money and success. In the chapter called, significantly enough, 'Hollow Men', Barney and Dan meet in a restaurant to discuss Barney's involvement with Caro; and the situation typifies the malaise afflicting both men: 'The place seemed full of people like us: klatsches of men, very few women, talking business, doing deals... middle-aged men hustling each other or preparing to hustle the world outside'. (*DM*, pp.273, 277) Placing the two in this context to discuss a personal relationship suggests that, for men like them, personal relationships themselves are a matter of hustling, a reproduction at the local level of the wider social relations perpetrated by their business world. Dan and Barney are mirror images of each other: though Dan is angry with Barney for taking up with and using his daughter Caro, he himself is in an identical situation with Jenny, also young enough to be his daughter. Dan has 'an uncomfortable feeling, like finding oneself in the same cell, and for the same crime, as a man one repudiated on every other ground.' (*DM*, p.275) It is not simply the two men but what they represent, the world of business manipulation and its values in which people are saleable commodities for other people's dreams, that is under scrutiny. Dan's 'self-disillusionment' puts him, as he recognises, 'in the same boat' as Barney and the others (*DM*, p.280), men for whom the values of their fathers, 'all the stabilising moral and religious values in society, were vanishing into thin air' (*DM*, p.279) precisely at the point when they themselves were ready to accept and pursue power and careers. The subsequent crisis for these men is registered at its most acute through Dan since, by his own admission, he is one of the most self-obsessed of his generation and, as a result of his father's influence, most sensitive to the erosion of belief and commitment. Dan's awareness of how the world he inhabits is infested by 'the glamorization of the worthless, the flagrant prostitution of true human values' (*DM*, p.279) puts him in constant contradiction with his use of that world for money and pleasure.

The appropriateness of the mass media and cinema as instruments to critically expose capitalism and masculinity lies exactly in this. Both enforce an economic exploitation through the manipulation of fantasy and imagery. From her neo-Marxist perspective, Jane voices a suspicion which Dan himself has long held about the dominant media. She regards 'TV and Fleet Street liberalism as the nastiest right-wing conspiracy yet', arguing 'I don't see why the cleverest have to be the most corrupt. And devote so much of their cleverness to perpetuating social and genetic advantage.' (*DM*, p.205) This is one element in her wider judgement on western society's wrong values, which, though she never specifically voices feminist arguments, inevitably connects with Dan's self-indictment of his own role as male scriptwriter. Dan himself 'had long begun to smell something rotten in the state of both these dominant media [film and television]; a little, perhaps, as an otherwise dutiful German official might once have begun to wonder about the Nazi Party. I had begun to see something ominously stereotyping, if not yet positively totalitarian, in the machine and its servants.' (*DM*, p.293) It is exactly this stereotyping capacity, typecasting in order to enforce power through falsification, that the book suggests is shared by both capitalism and male power. Indeed, through the cinema metaphor, the two are presented as interactive and synonymous. Jane tells Dan how Gramsci suggested that, under the 'ideological hegemony' of capitalism, 'Everything becomes reified, human beings become commodities, to be bought and sold. Mere objects, market research statistics—things to be manipulated by images'. (*DM*, p.418) In Dan's filmscript, Jenny gives herself to 'The Prick' as a sexual commodity in order to sell the film they are making as the fulfilment of male fantasies which produce profit. The illusions of male ideology and capitalist ideology jointly impose the social and economic prerogatives of the dominantly male business world with its ethic of competitive success, using people as ciphers of the media money-machine. Dan knows himself to be part of 'one of the audience-manipulating media' (*DM*, p.277), 'on the grab for quick success and cheap limelight' (*DM*, p.154). His problem is a sense of nausea at his own role but a seeming incapacity to escape it. We see this in his job as a scriptwriter and the fatal attraction its power holds.

This aspect of the book functions in a number of ways, but most interestingly it indicates the way Dan, like Urfe, imposes sexual scripts based on a male outlook on both women and himself. The literal manipulations of his profession as scriptwriter act as an analogy for his personal relations. The world of the filmscript is one of surface imagery and imposed illusion. Though aware from the first that 'cinema could never be as serious for me as the theatre' (*DM*, p.156), Dan's involvement with scriptwriting quickly becomes an extension of his power and freedom, 'by which he principally meant, though he hardly admitted it to himself, the freedom to exploit his growing success' (*DM*, p.150). The appeal of this power for his ego has its counterpart in the sexual power which he discovers success makes available. Dan is enmeshed in a world of self-compromise and betrayals, a world whose limits are defined and promoted by masculinity. His role almost inevitably becomes that of the flighty male, moving from one short-term affair to another, exploiting the pleasures of success in economic and sexual terms. The contradiction is his increasing awareness that the brittle surface masks a hollow interior. Like his scripts, his life acts out one dream after another. Though he feels that 'I had the compromises, the false pressures and premises of the film world in perspective' (*DM*, p.156), the unreality and prestige trap him into a series of parts, none of which satisfy him. His marriage was a mistake, a metaphorical, and then literal, 'production' (*DM*, p.156). Film is worse than theatre, since it 'betrays the real thing' (*DM*, p.20). It's function is 'peddling opium to the intellectually deprived' (*DM*, p.591), but feeling himself 'proof to the drug, he could allow himself to go on manufacturing it' (*DM*, p.293-4). The link between the male exploitation of power and sex roles is made in relation to Dan's marriage to Nell: 'The age of self offered him old sins he could convert into supposed new freedoms. It set her in a cage. That was her real jealousy; and his real adultery.' (*DM*, p.171)

One of his supposed new freedoms is sexual and its nature is highlighted by the terms in which Dan's first infidelity after marriage is put: 'Circe claimed she had a script she wanted Ulysses to read, if he was free for lunch.' (*DM*, p.149) Dan follows the stereotypical mythic patterns written into the male script but, though this analogy suggests such behaviour is historically general, the whole drive of the book is to show the *specific* conditions making up masculine attitudes and power within a particular society and its time. An example of this is offered by Dan's account of his relations with the two sisters, Miriam and Marjory, part of the 'swinging sixties'. In Dan's eyes, they brought him a temporary demonstration of the possibility of an ideal future relationship between men and women 'free of all the encumbrance, the suppuration, the vile selfishness of romantic love' (*DM*, p.269), 'a lasting lesson on the limitations of my class, my education and my kind' (*DM*, p.270). It is seemingly a utopian episode in his life, an idyll of the permissive society and an indication of his openness to forward-looking views; but behind it lurks the more realistic possibility articulated by Jenny—that it is just another example of the 'loathsome way you use other people's games to play your own' (*DM*, p.270). The encounter is presented notably through the critical metaphor of Dan as scriptwriter. The sisters apply for parts in a film and Dan 'saw a way of using them, then several ways; a potentiality of development' (*DM*, p.257). He does indeed find several ways of using them, sleeping first with one sister then with the other in a flexible ménage à trois. When suddenly they leave, they linger for him in his memory as emblems and muses: 'They taunt, they live, and I envy with all my heart every man who has had them since.' (*DM*, p.271) This dubious note undercuts the supposed progressiveness of Dan's viewpoint with contradictions similar to those identified by feminists as typical of 'progressive' men in the late 1960s who preached sexual liberation on male terms. Similarly, Dan is little or no different in 'the kind of man he is from the vulgarest kind of vanity, the Casanova aspect of the beast; from the notched tally, the quite literal cocksureness' (*DM*, p.255), merely more refined in his form of exploitation.

The scriptwriter theme then, as a critical metaphor, exposes the monopoly of power shared by masculinity and capitalism. Realistically, one expects Dan's redemption from this world, his commitment to the 'real' (to use the term increasingly introduced into his narrative) to be a process bedevilled with contradictions. To reveal these Fowles exploits to the full the notion of the book as Dan's own construction, effectively attempting a totalised account of the social and historical processes impinging on this individual psyche. In this sense, the book is an unearthing of the reasons for Dan's present self, an archaeological investigation of his identity as a man. This is quite literally so since the method of the narrative is to interleaf sections from different parts of Dan's life, showing them like accumulated strata beneath the contours of his psychological landscape. This methodology is presented as Dan's own choice of narrative mode in his turning from the illusory world of film to the novel as a truer medium for composing experience. It is his arrangement of experience, a point made clear on a number of occasions, most notably in the 'Tsankawi' chapter. Writing there in the first person, Dan says that the 'first seed of what this book is trying to be dropped into my mind that day: a longing for a medium that would tally better with this real structure of my racial being and mind... something dense, interweaving, treating time as horizontal, like a skyline; not cramped, linear and progressive.' (*DM*, p.353) At other points, we get not simply the sense of Dan describing his gropings towards the new medium of the novel, but the intercutting of a present 'writerly' self actually composing the text. After the episode of the two sisters, Dan says 'I can hear them sniff-and-giggle if they ever read this.' (*DM*, p.269) To explain the inclusion of the chapter called 'The Sacred Combe', Dan describes how this was the seed for the book's genesis: it was 'the ghost of a central character, a theme, of a thing in the mind that might once more make reality the metaphor and itself the reality... a more difficult truth about the invention of myths than he had had the courage to tell Caro'. Thus, 'Spending a page or two on it is not quite outraging versimilitude' (*DM*, p.288), all of which invokes a self-explaining author as the book's character.

The novel, then, presents itself as Dan's attempt to analyse and reconstitute himself, to lay the ghosts of his past. The intercutting of time and narratives is the filmscript writer's method of creating his own *bildüngsroman* through montage and collage. It also represents Dan's commitment to escaping the world of the camera and the script, of surface appearances and 'lying' (*DM*, p.292) in favour of the Gramscian apprehension of totality, the 'Whole sight' advocated in the very first sentence of the book (*DM*, p.7) and impressed upon him by Anthony as the only salvation (*DM*, p.196). This commitment is also his rejection of his previous involvement in the manipulations of capitalism and male power, and the dominant narrative mode of neo-Lukácsian social realism demonstrates an engagement with the 'real' which becomes an important thematic element. Despite the chinese-box overlap,

Fowles's adoption of Dan as surrogate author allows him a detachment through which he can analyse the very contradictions which he himself is subject to as a male writer, seeing the process of writing and self-analysis as part of the problem he wishes to specify. This procedure is one of the book's main achievements but it is not without its difficulties.

Jenny proposes the name 'Simon Wolfe' for her fictional version of Dan, an obviously Fowlesian pun, being an anagram of Fowles's own name as Conradi points out.[7] Dan appropriates her suggestion and develops it by talking about himself in the third person; but his book remains a fictional 'reconstruction' (*DM*, 256) which is biased from his point of view. He decides, for example, to 'recast' Jenny's contributions and censors her third one describing their visit to Tsankawi (*DM*, p.346). In itself, his novel-writing thus remains a contradictory business despite its apparent sense of commitment since, even in the novel 'As every Marxist critic has pointed out, this withdrawal from outer fact into inner fantasy is anti-social and inherently selfish', the pursuit of more mirrors to reflect the self (*DM*, p.294). Is it 'self-accountancy—or escape' (*DM*, p.429)? It is a point Fowles himself is by now pertinently aware of and we may presume that this suggestion that we should not trust Daniel Martin's fiction applies to his creator too. In order to indicate his *own* attention to this process of male bias active in fiction, Fowles focuses our attention on the ambivalent slippage between 'I' and 'he' which keeps entering Dan's novel, a prevarication of pronouns which counterpoints the deviousness of Dan's male persona and his attempts to distance or escape it.

It is not simply a matter of Dan as a writer having a certain critical removal from his past self, indicating, as in Urfe's case, a degree of development. This comes into it of course, as in this comment by Dan on his Oxford self: 'He had one virtue, I suppose. He read other people's moods fast;... but only the moods, not the intentions.' (*DM*, p.61) Fowles's strategy goes further, however. It shows Dan as writer both detaching himself from his past behaviour and continuing to confuse himself with it, distinguishing the role of the male 'he' from the more authentic 'I' and then reimposing them on each other. It suggests that, in his attempt at 'distinguishing between his actual self and a hypothetical fictional projection of himself' (*DM*, p.427), Dan has only partially succeeded. The detachment is incomplete and it is the gender element in the pronoun shift from 'I' to 'he' that shows the role he cannot escape. It is 'I' who invites Jane to go to Egypt for the cruise, but 'Then he began to wonder what he had done.' (*DM*, p.426) Dan explains 'Neither the first nor the third person that he also was wanted Jane in his arms again' (*DM*, p.437), but it is patently self-deception. The awkwardness of this narrative tactic suggests the anxiety provoked in Daniel over his sense of self and, familiarly, it is Jane who forces this splitting in him:

> It was almost a heuristic quality. Even when she was being thoughtless, she made him think... increasingly he knew it was of value to him, to both of him, Daniel Martin and 'Simon Wolfe'. His *métier* had forced him for so long to think in terms of visual symbolism, of sets, locations, movements, gestures; of the seen actor and actress. This psychologically obscure creature belonged, or had grown to belong, to another art, another system, the one he was trying to enter.
>
> Above all he had to distinguish his real self from his putative fictional one; and though his training in an adamantly third-person art and angle of vision might seem to facilitate such auto-surgery, he felt deeply unsure about it. There too he had an apprehension that Jane could help—that the 'making him think' was essentially a making him look at himself through her eyes. (*DM*, p.441)

What Fowles shows through this unwieldy but fascinating technique is the process of change in the self, and the contradictions consequent on it. Dan is neither fully an 'I' free of gender roles, nor merely a chauvinistic 'he' untouched by other values. He is caught between the two, living out an inward ambiguity which, as the form of the book indicates by the slippages, he has not been able to resolve. Inevitably, Fowles himself comes within the frame of the same critique even in the process of elevating it to 'a principle of knowledge and therefore of action'.

There are distinct risks involved in the venture of analysing Dan's attempt to analyse himself. The limits of Dan's self-analysis are exactly its self-absorption, the extent of which borders on the infuriating or tedious. The intellectualising, the introspective soul-searching, the overt attempts to psychologise and construct schematic arrangements of experience are to be seen for what they are—the lingering self-concern of a man whose life has been geared to that very object, symptomatic of Dan's malaise rather than a lapse on Fowles's part. The precariousness of this is something Fowles seems to have been well aware of. In his interview with Donald Hall he said that the book had weak passages almost as a matter of policy: 'I have always liked in novels a fluctuating quality. I find it attractive; I think that sometimes boring passages are quite important.'[8] This tendentiousness of Dan even allows Fowles the occasional joke, as in the chapter called 'Webs' where Dan feels 'like someone locked up inside an adamantly middle-class novel; a smooth, too plausible Establishment fixer out of C.P. Snow, not a lone wolf at all' (DM, p.246). The script that neither Fowles nor his male surrogate can easily escape, as the 'I'/'he' tension suggests, is the social legacy of masculinity at the individual level. To indicate this, part of Daniel's digging back into his past involves confronting two key mythical monsters in his unconscious which bar this errant knight's quest for his grail—his father and mother.

In the retrospective first chapter the young Dan is already 'nursing his solitude, his terrible Oedipal secret; already at the crossroads every son must pass' (DM, p.15). Describing his underhand escape from Jenny, he explains 'I suppose the experience with Nell formed me there, no doubt on a predisposed Freudian pattern.' (DM, p.73) One element in the pattern results from that classic patriarchal paradigm which Fowles sees as the dynamic for his own creative impulse, the desire for the lost mother; but in this book he adds that key element in the equation which is merely hinted at in the other novels—fear of the father.

What Dan discovers about his relation to his father is the ambivalent legacy of patriarchal power which is the root of his masculine identity. He recognises that his father conditioned him 'by antithesis' (DM, p.83). All the things his father represented for him as a child he realises he reacted against and buried from sight; but as he reaches a point of crisis later in the book he begins to wonder 'whether he hadn't been formed in his father's image and in a sense not too far removed from that father's God and *his* son;

almost, that is, for a secret paternal purpose, though in Dan's case it would be more accurately called a paternal defect.' (*DM*, p.503) Fowles gives a comic demonstration of this phallic inheritance in the chapter called 'The Umbrella'. Dan remembers his father's repression of 'any nakedness of feeling' (*DM*, p.84), his faith in 'order', the 'totally accepted belief in the system, the existing social frame' (*DM*, pp.85-6). This belief in the established hierarchy made him 'a subtle—rather than classic—example of why the military and the ecclesiastical, cross and sword, so often seem just two faces of the same coin.' (*DM*, p.85) The conservativism and moral stricture, legacies of Victorian middle-class patriarchal values, are inescapably part of his father's formative influence on Dan despite their being useless and despised encumbrances. This contradiction, the mark of the phallus, is dramatised in the umbrella episode itself. Dan is left to carry his father's umbrella, emblem of the archaic shelter of an outmoded belief system, and he feels a number of reactions including humiliation, resentment and hate. He is mortified by the incident, partly because it takes place in front of the girl Margaret. It serves to indicate both his separation from his father and, contradictorily, his adoption of his father's position. Dan might reject the overt forms of his father's belief in order, morals and so on, but this rejection itself determines the make-up of his own masculine identity in 'negative' (*DM*, p.86). The repression of feeling by his father and the early death of Dan's mother lead Dan to a recurrent desire to make himself metaphorically and literally naked to women, his tendency to be 'congenitally unfaithful' (*DM*, p.189). His repudiation of his father's moral discipline leads him 'to shed unnecessary guilt, irrational respect, emotional dependence' (*DM*, p.95), with the result that relationships seem relative and impermanent to him. Yet though he rejected success in his father's terms, he was 'like every other middle-class child, educated to see life in terms of success in examinations and games' (*DM*, p.289) at the school to which his father sends him. There he discovered 'new aspects of myself; an inventiveness, even though it most often manifested itself as a skill in lying; a tongue, an extrovert mask. I also wanted to succeed, with a ferocity that might not have been predicted of my earlier years.' (*DM*, p.92) In terms which anticipate his later views on the cinema, Dan describes how he loathed team games at school: 'I thought at the time it was merely because they were an obvious emblem of the whole sadistically stereotyping system. But I see now it was one more negative way in which father and his world-outlook conditioned me.' (*DM*, p.86)

Behind all the reactions against his father, there remains one common factor between them, a desire for control, for a certain order. Dan himself has 'a hatred of change, of burning boats' (*DM*, p.576). He is caught 'between two things he fears, emotion and unreason' (*DM*, p.49) when he gets the unexpected call from Jane. His forms of control in manipulating his success in terms of career and sexual relations, however different from his father's, are nevertheless the same in kind, forms of male power. It is a power Dan himself felt the victim of at a crucial moment in adolescence, when his father decreed his separation from Nancy Reed, a metaphoric castration which enforces the imperative of male power and law on Dan. This was the real 'severance' from his father (*DM*, p.92), a severance which confirms the antithetical influence of patriarchy rather than denying it. Faced by his father's command not to see Nancy again, Dan knew he was 'trapped by convention, by respectability, by class, by Christianity, by the ubiquitous wartime creed of discipline and self-restraint as the ultimate goods. But the worst of all was knowing that I had asked for this terrible disaster. I believed in God again that night; he had my father's face and I cried with my loathing of his power.' (*DM*, p.403) It is a castration crisis which, in the eyes of Lacanian analysts of masculinity, is the point of confirmation of male identity, the point at which the male child takes up his position with the father through fear and a desire to wield the same power.[9]

Dan's attempt to resolve this legacy is initially to find his own power in the form of career and relationships. His attitudes to these interconnect, as we have seen, delineating the contours of his male behaviour. He realises that his father and himself have one thing in common, a desire for safety which they can regulate:

> Never mind that Dan had rebelled against such timidity in countless outward ways, he still strove, even in the shifting nows of his life, always for control, a safe place. The nature of his work, his frequent experience of beginning a new script before the last one was fully realized, was paralleled in his private life, in the way he would so often think himself out of relationships with women long before they actually ended. That might seem to argue against a desire for stasis. But perhaps it was simply that the old man had found—by hazard and unthinkingly, since Christianity in this context was no more than the answer to a fear—what his son was searching for. Dan's solution had been, like some kinds of animal, to find safety in movement... Yet somehow this seemed a very superficial paradox between father and son. In both cases there was a same flaw of nature: a need not to question, to ban certain possibilities. (*DM*, p.503)

Underlying the psychology of both father and son lies the same defensive insecurity which necessitates the same desire for control, the conservativism of the male which Fowles argues in *The Aristos*.

It is for this reason that Fowles includes the figure of Kitchener in Dan's story, the 'hangrope round the writer's neck' (*DM*, p.297) and his final script. In this sense Kitchener is the ghost of patriarchy haunting Dan's life. This might seem rather far-fetched, but in fact this is how Dan himself comes to regard this archetype of late nineteenth-century imperialism. Confronting Kitchener becomes a correlative for confronting both his father and his own masculine drive for power. As the challenge which Jane poses to his masculine identity becomes more overt, he begins to realise that 'the real scenario that was haunting him was not Kitchener's, but his own' (*DM*, p.576). This comes at a point in the book when Jane is talking to a young Egyptian girl of whom Dan approves sexually: he 'even jumped on to finding some tiny part for her in the film, in his early days Kitchener must have been offered such creatures'. The equation between the film, Dan's own manipulations of women and the patriarchal values epitomised by Kitchener, 'the shrewd old self-promoter' (*DM*, p.545), shows how Dan, while rejecting Kitchener's nationalism, carries on the legacy of male imperialism.

Capitalism, imperialism, chauvinism, success, manipulation, the whole world of male imagery and power which Fowles locates in the notion of film-making, perpetrate a one-sided view of the world in order to perpetuate that power. This is the 'Devil' which

Anthony identifies, the devil of 'Not seeing whole' (*DM*, p.196). Anthony's death-bed repentance, his attempt to correct 'a design failure' (*DM*, p.186) by revealing to Dan that Jane had confessed about their sleeping together, is significant in this respect. Anthony is asking absolution for *his* having manipulated their lives and made Jane his 'victim' (*DM*, p.188) in the sense that, as becomes apparent, she felt obliged to sacrifice herself by marrying Anthony because of her 'gratuitous act' (*DM*, p.99). By comparison with Anthony's emotional blackmail, at least Dan has 'rationed out [his] exploitations' (*DM*, p.189). The problem posed in the novel is for Dan to begin to realise how he implements the power legacy of patriarchy and actively abdicate from it. The father may give way to the son, but male power remains more or less intact. The king is dead; long live the king—or, as Dan's father put it at the end of the umbrella episode in the only joke he ever made to his son, 'I have lost a son. But I have found a gargoyle.' (*DM*, p.98)

The other crucial element in the Freudian paradigm, of course, is the lost mother, whose death is figured in the female corpse Dan and Jane discover while out boating and whose absence motivates Dan's pursuit of the various women in his life as the emotional supplement to his inadequacies and power. In the chapter called 'Interlude', Dan's uncomfortableness in the company of other men is seen as the corollary to his search for new 'encounters' with women: 'He had very rarely sought male company for pleasure, perhaps because it threatened his always precarious sense of uniqueness. He saw himself too easily in other masculine faces, mannerisms, machismos, ambitions, failings.' (*DM*, p.255) Other men remind Dan of the ambivalence of his masculine identity and the precariousness underlying its motives. His relationships with women allow him power and emotional support by bolstering his sense of 'uniqueness': 'his real attitude there was at least partly, he would say centrally, botanical... It was not categorizing and counting, but searching. He liked looking for women who would interest him, for new specimens.' (*DM*, p.255) Dan too is a collector and what he shares with Clegg is this same seeing of women in relation to his own ego. His needs are not specifically sexual and he 'always despised, or more latterly, pitied, the men for whom he knew it was.' His form of vanity is to use women to reflect himself, and he traces this narcissism back to its Freudian roots as a search for a pre-Oedipal unity, a self-sufficiency contradictorily dependent on the primal figure of chidlhood:

> He was arguably not even looking for women in all this, but collecting mirrors still; surfaces before which he could make himself naked—or at any rate more naked than he could before other men—and see himself reflected. A psychoanalyst might say he was searching for the lost two-in-one identity of his first months of life; some solution for his double separation trauma, the universal one of infancy and the private experience of literally losing his mother. (*DM*, pp.255-6)

All his relations with women are manipulative attempts to script them into the role of surrogate for the lost mother, to fulfil the deficiencies which Dan's masculine legacy forces on him for all its power. It is the key to the connection the novel offers between the image world of film and the world of male power. Both manipulate through fantasy and in doing so, they reproduce male prerogatives according to the 'script' of masculinity. As Dan realises about Jenny, 'I suppose I was also looking, as all men do, for a sacrifice of her real self, or at least of all the parts of it that conflicted with the more concealed elements of my own.' (*DM*, p.355)

Jenny's role in the book in showing up this hidden agenda is crucial, since her contributions are one central lever in Dan's prising open of his old self; and here we must distinguish the book as Dan supposedly sees it from the book as it is to be read. For him Jenny represents the 'unreal', the imagined world of fantasy and illusion from which he wishes to abdicate. What Jenny does is to indicate how far Dan still is from his envisaged redemption with Jane, and how that redemption itself is a realignment of his power. She acts as his scourge.

Her view of him becomes progressively more bitter. It is Dan who, on hearing Jane's lover has found someone else in America, says 'Men are shits' (*DM*, p.411), but it is Jenny who proves it about himself. As in Urfe's relationship with Alison, Dan has the proverbial upper hand over Jenny. He begins by seeming the more vulnerable, as with his defensive comment to her about love being 'a sickness' of his generation which he does not expect her to catch (*DM*, p.48). It is reminiscent of G.P.'s similar tactics with Miranda and it soon becomes apparent that Dan has long ago relegated 'the ridiculous décors of the heart' (*DM*, p.55) to the status of stage props. For Jenny, though she appears to him as one of a liberated generation, her emotional needs are something she cannot honestly deny, unlike Dan. As he increasingly flirts with his hidden mistress 'Loss' (*DM*, p.251), so Jenny increasingly realises that she loves him and her honesty is used to castigate his deviousness. The lies with which he surrounds their relationship are readily exposed: the first, concerning the casting for the script Jenny is acting in (*DM*, p.69), forms a metaphor of the general situation. Dan's lying about Steve not being the first choice for the male part in the film seems to Jenny 'like your practising all you claim you hate in Hollywood: fool the stupid broad, never mind what lies you tell her as long as she gives a better performance.' (*DM*, p.461) Dan wants Jenny to play a part in his life as well as in his film, but only on terms he can control. Thus, though she realises that he is 'in ruins somewhere' (*DM*, p.19), he won't give her enough information about his past for him to begin feeling vulnerable or dependent on her. He lies about why he is going back to England after the phone call (*DM*, p.53), saying nothing about Jane. He lies to Jane about the significance of Jenny in his life, demoting her in an appallingly dismissive remark to the status of 'just a carpet hung up to keep out the wind' (*DM*, p.624). The lie in this case is not about his own feelings, for he goes on quite honestly to say 'I can't go on using her like that. Apart from anything else, she knows it.' (*DM*, p.624) The deception is in his reductive presentation of his own significance for Jenny, a manipulation designed to make him appear to Jane as in a position permitting a break with Jenny for her. Dan recognises how involved he is in 'the prevarication business' (*DM*, p.244), the theme of the English tendency to adopt masks summed up in the Robin Hood myth (*DM*, p.289). For Jenny, Dan is eventually just another clichéd male, 'a devious, lying bastard' (*DM*, p.655): 'I know your game. We're all so much easier to live with when we're just notions in your past. I think you're the original male chauvinist pig.' (*DM*, p.657)

It is important to register how central Jenny's criticism is, since it has a direct bearing on the way he casts Jane as the redemptive enigmatic woman in his novel. It is not for nothing that Jenny chooses the name 'Wolfe' for her fictional version of Dan. It allows Fowles another literary joke when Jenny says 'you can't use your own name in a novel. Anyway, its so square. Who'd ever go for a character called Daniel Martin?' (*DM*, p.23); but it also points up the association with that familiar male cliché, the lone wolf, 'Something solitary. Devious' (*DM*, p.23) and predatory. It is a role Dan acts out and is trapped by, as well as using it to exploit others. In Jenny's eyes he would at times 'come on a shade too urbane (this is in public). The much-travelled man of the world and all that. On the other hand (as he knows) I hate men who can't handle hotels, restaurants, waiters—success life, if you have to lead it. I suppose doing it well inevitably means role-playing.' (*DM*, p.37) He is quite ready to cast himself in those very terms, as in his reductive image of himself and Jenny as acting out 'the ravings of the male menopause and a naked film-star in Harold Robbins Land' (*DM*, p.21). He knows that there is 'the old lone wolf, the hater of encumbrance in him; of the effort, the energy and time and diplomacy involved in walking the tightrope between all these contradictory female faces and forces in his present life' and he dreams of 'that very ancient male dream embodied in Mount Athos and its monasteries' (*DM*, p.484), a monkish isolation away from women. For Jenny, all his contradictions amount to is a 'foul double-dealing' (*DM*, p.457), 'what male rats have said ever since time began' (*DM*, p.454), and she decides 'I just won't be *only* something in your script. In any of your scripts. Ever again.' (*DM*, p.471)

In this respect, Jenny realises that the hidden figure in the carpet of Dan's psychology is Jane herself, the key surrogate for Dan's lost mother since she re-enacted the pattern of being possessed and lost in marrying Anthony. As Jenny tells Dan at the end of the book, 'I can see there were always casting problems. With us pale shadows who offered for the part.' (*DM*, p.663) What the narrative strategies of Fowles's book show is that Jane's revived role in Dan's life is exactly that, still a role in his patriarchal script, recast as it is into the novel form, the role of enigma, redeemer and substitute mother. Dan shows himself struggling to escape from imposing this pattern, whilst Fowles shows how contradictory such a struggle by a male author is.

As a measure of her potential to break the old stereotypes, Jane's first words on meeting Dan are 'I've forgotten my lines.' (*DM*, p.163) From the first, he feels distance and uncomfortableness with her, but perhaps for this very reason she soon becomes seen as the emblem of his lost self, the lost domaine. His awareness that his marriage to Nell was a mistake (*DM*, p.160), is counterpoised by his sense that he should have married Jane (*DM*, p.177), and that if he had he 'might have been a better writer, or at least a less transient playwright' (*DM*, p.361). Dan's inclination for seeking solutions from women lead him to start seeing Jane as 'some kind of emblem of a redemption from a life devoted to heterogamy and adultery, the modern errant ploughman's final reward' (*DM*, p.596). As in *The French Lieutenant's Woman*, the central contradiction in this is that the salvation Jane offers, if any, is far from consolatory. It is posed as a challenge to abandon self-gratification, to accept insecurity, to abandon power and Fowles shows Daniel exploring his own struggle to come to terms with these imperatives. In doing so, both character-author and actual author are inevitably involved in a manipulation of Jane as a symbolic figure.

While at Thornecombe Dan takes Jane to see his mother's grave and realises 'this obscure ex-sister-in-law was someone whose spirit remained not quite like that of any other woman he had ever known; that there are some people one can't dismiss, place, reify... who set riddles one ignores at one's cost' (*DM*, p.440). Fowles peppers Daniel's narrative with the all-too-familiar features of the Fowlesian mystery woman with the twist that this time we are onlookers on her casting for the part Dan wishes her to play in his fiction: 'I felt confirmed in seeking some clue in Jane that might be central to what I wanted to write myself' (*DM*, p.321), he reflects. Her 'heuristic quality' (*DM*, p.441) as it seems to him disrupts his sense of self and offers at the same time a renewal, an escape from his sense of being 'in exile from what I ought to have been' (*DM*, p.20). She seems to offer another mirror but 'she was also unique in not mirroring him clearly... She still, as she always had, disturbed images, changed voices, recast scenes' (*DM*, p.441). This attribution of power to Jane by Dan is shown as a fictional idealisation in action and part of what he has to learn to come to terms with. In Dan's fictional scheme, Jenny is the 'imagined' (*DM*, p.447), the product of a world of illusions, whereas Jane is the 'real' or, more precisely, 'something in Jane's presence satisfied some deep need in me of recurrent structure in both real and imagined events; indeed, married the real and imagined; justified both' (*DM*, p.422). Notably it is his 'deep need' that receives priority.

This formulation comes in that crucial episode when Dan offers to take Jane to Egypt. Significantly, it is a moment at which her political critique of his world is at its strongest: 'I just feel that our society has got so blind. So selfish. It's all I can ever see nowadays. And the only people who could change anything, change it intelligently, do absolutely nothing about it. Refuse to give up anything. Share anything.' (*DM*, p.412) Dan's response is to offer her the temptation of opting out of the struggle: 'Perhaps that's the answer. Cultivate your garden.' (*DM*, p.415) Increasingly fascinated by what he sees as her 'mystery' (*DM*, p.420), for him 'the bizarre political step' of her joining the Communist Party is merely a 'substitute' for some other, more satisfying commitment (*DM*, p.421). The point is that as Jane's challenge to his power grows stronger, so Dan's reaction is to contain it by transforming her into an idealised sphinx who holds the key to his future, a future predicated in his terms of a personal relationship between them rather than in terms of her political vision. He sees her merely as the catalyst subserving his own fiction writing: 'She was like an old enigma in his life, and she had to be solved; tamed and transcribed. Perhaps, though once again he did not think this consciously... she had some kind of kinship with the Kitchener script: a problem to crack, to be converted to another medium, though in the emotions, not on the page.' (*DM*, p.430) It is here that 'he came to the most important decision of his life', one which 'though it may seem a supremely self-centred declaration, it is in fact a supremely socialist one.' (*DM*, p.431) The decision is his commitment to novel-writing and the rejection of the film world. The note of self-justification indicates the contradiction Fowles wants to pinpoint, the fantasising tendencies of the male novelist masquerading as social commitment, and this contradiction becomes increasingly fraught as the book shows Dan more and more desperate to contain Jane in the mythical role he has imagined for her.

By the time they reach Luxor on their Egyptian trip, Dan feels that the relationship between them, far from holding the possibility of a romantic fulfilment, is vitiated by a baffling reserve, a perverse evasion of the accepted rules of the game. As author, he shows himself aware of how his resentment at Jane's reserve manufactured itself from the limits of his own psychology: it 'betrayed a retardation in himself; a quasi-Freudian searching for the eternally lost, his vanished mother. There too, as with his father, he was much more deeply conditioned than he could easily admit. Something in him must always look for that, even in much younger women. . . All his close relationships with women. . . were variations on the model; and broke down precisely because they could not support what his unconscious demanded of them.' He resolves to break this absurd 'repetition compulsion': 'I must start treating this woman as she is.' (*DM*, p.513) What Daniel the author shows is how, having reached this point of self-awareness, Daniel the character struggles ineffectually to put his new resolution into practice in the face of the disconcerting shift in relations that Jane brings. What Fowles shows is how Daniel the author is himself far from having eradicated these key patterns structuring his male identity through his unconscious, for the role Jane plays in his book remains that of the enigmatic muse though in these new, Fowlesian terms.

It is noticeable how, true to this resolve, Daniel is shown making a deliberate effort not to impose his feelings on Jane; and equally, how frustrated he becomes in the process. The key to this lies in the critical point that while Dan sees Jane as a way out of his own cul-de-sac, she, like Sarah, views a renewed relationship as a trap. He explains her reserve and mystery quite egocentrically as relating to himself, when in fact at a number of points we see Jane trying to communicate the predicament *she* is in: 'you do have an interesting career, Dan. It really is rather different for us. My kind of woman. At my age.' (*DM*, p.414) 'I understand how you feel about your work', she tells him in relation to his sense of disillusion, 'But I don't even have that. A direction ahead.' (*DM*, pp.574-5)

Her problem is deeper than that, however, and embraces a need for autonomy which verges on an argument for separatism, overtly threatening Dan's desire for a renewed relationship. Whilst he is fantasising her as 'an emblem of redemption' (*DM*, p.596) and trying to argue her into accepting a continuing involvement, her response is 'I have so little to give' and it makes him feel like 'the swimmer who knew the sea would be cold, but still finds it colder than the foreknowledge' (*DM*, p.598). He asserts that 'The last thing I'd want is to stop you living as you like' (*DM*, p.600) but, behind the liberalism, there is the conservativism of the male commitment to the heterosexual couple as a way of maintaining a hold over women. It is a point of crisis specific to the anxieties felt by men of the 1970s[10] and one which Fowles captures in Daniel as an attempt to realign his power in order to keep Jane from too extreme a revolt. When he almost literally proposes to her—'I'd just like us to try living together. For better or for worse'—he is clearly dislocated by her lack of enthusiasm, and asks 'since when was it a time when women needed solitude?' (*DM*, p.600) Inadvertently, he stumbles over the reason why he seems cut off behind 'a pane of glass; but unbreakable glass' (*DM*, p.601), though it is left to her to spell it out: 'You've had so much freedom, Dan. You choose prison just as I'm trying to leave it.' After her sacrificial marriage to Anthony, 'love is a prison': 'I'm not nearly as independent as you imagine. That's why I feel I have to cling to what little I have.' (*DM*, p.602)

Daniel's response to this fundamental argument exemplifies his struggle to contain this threatening autonomy. He falls back on emotional blackmail: 'the knight is just as much in distress as the damsel' (*DM*, p.603), he tells her picking up on the image from the end of *The French Lieutenant's Woman* (*FLW*, p.381), a point which relates to the intriguing fact that Fowles's original idea for the opening chapter of *Daniel Martin* was to set it in the back lot of Warner Brothers studios with the decaying set from 'Camelot' still in place.[11] It is of a piece with Daniel's own male myth, the 'mythical true marriage' (*DM*, p.216) between himself and Jane which her marriage to Anthony prevented. In a moment of highly ambiguous honesty, he admits:

> Men like me can always find sex and new female minds to play with. What I need from you is that something inside you, between us, that makes half-living, half-loving like that impossible... Jenny McNeil knows she's being used, she's as objective and open about it as... as any intelligent girl of her generation. Brutally honest about how she sees me. But then goes on letting herself be used. Which relegates me to the status of interesting experience. In terms of your new religion, she and I both reify each other. Become characters in a fiction. Forget how to see each other totally. So we invent roles, play games, to hide the gap. I meet you again, I suddenly see all this, what was wrong from the beginning, why you were the one woman who might have led me out of it. (*DM*, p.603)

The seeming disingenuousness of this merely masks a more invidious kind of manipulation which seeks to put Jane inescapably into Dan's novel to fulfil his needs. It is a containment he struggles to effect in the face of set-backs which displace his behaviour and show them as the classic stereotypes of male ideology. After their disagreement he envisages a romantic resolution, 'a tap on his door, a standing there, a solution that would need no words; as it would happen in a script' (*DM*, pp.604-5), but Jane resolutely refuses to play this role while Dan cannot escape it. He feels jealous of Assad's attentions to her, for which he 'called himself a male chauvinist; but the self-accusation came from liberal convention, not personal conviction' (*DM*, p.608). He sees himself 'being burnt on the oldest of fires', hoping for 'an infantile happy-ever-after afterwards device from fairy tales, a ludicrous myth' (*DM*, p.609) to resolve his dilemma.

His liberal facade quickly falters in the hotel at Palmyra when he accuses her of having 'murdered' a possibility of their happiness in the past (*DM*, p.627) and effectively doing the same again: 'The one mystery to me', he says with his gloves well and truly off, 'is how I can have fallen twice in my life for such an impossible bitch of a woman.' (*DM*, p.629) Their sleeping together simply confirms for him 'the death of the illusion that they could find each other as simply as this', exploding the Lawrentian myth, while his sense of impotence extends beyond that as increasingly he feels 'outraged like a man before a machine that will not function, although he has followed to the letter all the instructions for starting it' (*DM*, p.641). Sex with her had been just 'an act of charity, a sop to his male esteem, a solitary fuck; just as his career had given him "success" in a world that also became lost ruins in a lost desert almost as soon as it was achieved.' (*DM*, p.645)

There are clear political implications behind this destruction of male mythologies in Daniel. Just as Jane offers Dan renewed authenticity in his estimation, so she enforces a move towards social or political commitment and the abdication of power, as Dan realises:

> Anyone intelligent who went in for the medium [of film] commercially must have a profound desire to limit his commitments, to whore after shifting gods; and this secret infatuation for a deeper relationship with far more than the ambiguous woman beside him went against every practical lesson he had learnt from life. That with Jane it would, if carried to a conclusion, lead to a closing of all kinds of sexual and career and domestic options worried him a great deal less than the prospect of an irreducible obstinacy, a permanent psychological awkwardness she would bring. (*DM*, p.591)

Jane's political leanings are the antithesis of Dan's involvement in business, power and male values, just as her need for separate autonomy denies his personal hold over her.

In this sense, though she challenges his containment of women she remains a corrective ideal in relation to the deficiencies of the male. When Dan is discussing Kitchener with the Tory MP Fenwick and with Andrew, he feels the absurdity of their reactionary talk, of the setting at Compton, of the men left after dinner to their cigars and brandy. Fenwick's brand of conservatism repulses him and he jokingly volunteers himself to Jane as a recruit for the Communist Party alongside her (*DM*, p.340). Yet he recognises that 'there must seem, to someone like Jane, a psychological similarity between us [i.e. between Dan, Fenwick and Andrew]; a shared malice of defeat... for all that I hid mine better.' (*DM*, p.339) Dan is part of the male ruling class as he ironically admits to Jane later, satirising his own privileges but merely succeeding in confirming them. Dan is lamenting the state of modern society:

'In a world where the future gets more horrible to contemplate every day?' She gave him a sceptical look. 'Oh yes. I travel. I write. I meet film-stars. I'm a very lucky fellow.' He added, 'The last of the ancient régime.'
His voice had been dry to the point of bitterness, and the delay in her answer underlined it.
'Then it is a privileged form of pessimism.'
'Of accidie. Powerlessness.'
'It's not very obvious, Dan.' (*DM*, p.592)

It is the disillusioned and self-pitying man, tired and not a little guilty of the profit of his freedom and power, seeking solace in another form of power, while the woman he has earmarked for the purpose is moving in the opposite direction. Daniel Martin as novelist now looks back on 'his oldest and worst self' as one of the 'morbid symptoms' of the 'interregnum' indicated in the epigram from Gramsci which accompanies the book's title page (*DM*, p.3):

> Like a spoilt child deprived of a toy, barred by his past and his present from feeling anything but eternally spoilt... excluded, castrated by both capitalism and socialism, forbidden to belong. Our hero, spurned by one side for not feeling happier, despised by the other for not feeling more despair; in neither a tragedy nor a comedy, but a bourgeois melodrama—that short-lived theatrical fad, as he sourly remembered, despatched into a deserved oblivion during the great crack-up of 1789. (*DM*, p.611)

This abdication of privilege in so far as Dan achieves it at all carries with it a potential realignment of power which the book indicates precisely by its containment of Jane within Dan's novel and the role she is made to play in it. We can see this contradiction most plainly in the way the book ends.

After the cathartic experience at Palmyra, when Dan receives from Jane 'his answer and his resolution' (*DM*, p.652), his 'fiction-making' is increasingly exposed for what it is. In the last chapter, ambiguously titled 'Future Past', Dan goes through the process of rejecting Jenny in order to commit himself to Jane. Not only does this allow for Jenny's castigation of Dan, as we have already mentioned, as 'the original male chauvinist pig' (*DM*, p.657); it shows him continuing to 'script' situations according to his own egocentric desires, actively backing up Jenny's view of him rather than encouraging a sense that he has changed:

'I suppose you've told her all about me.'

'All about why I never deserved you.'

'I wish you'd write a script about a woman who kills a man out of rage at the phoniness of his decency.' (*DM*, p.659)

His 'decency' here is phoney, after the dismissive description he gave of Jenny to Jane, and there is an internal smugness about him as when Jenny tells him '"I don't think you'll ever have the patience for a novel." He knew what she really meant by "novel"; but not how to answer without hurting her. "I bet you'll be back on scripts within six months."' (*DM*, p.658) Like a Calvinist, Dan seems to have this salvation cut and dried, but Jenny's reflection on his 'novel' reminds us how much of a manipulation that might also be. What he wants from Jenny in this final scene is again the upper hand, a reassurance for his ego which she actively denies him by leaving without allowing him the final word, and it reveals exactly how devious Dan is even at this point of supposed commitment:

> He stood watching her, feeling obscurely tricked, even in some way hurt that it had been her decision—which told him that it had been one that still, somewhere deep inside himself, he had not absolutely taken. . .
>
> He felt bereft beyond his calculation of it; almost cheated by the understanding of himself he had arrived at over the last two months, and which he had tried to convey to her; trapped in his own trap, turned someone he wasn't. (*DM*, p.666)

Despite his sheepish revelation that he is now 'a fully paid-up member of the Labour Party' (*DM*, p.664), Dan is still hedging his emotional bets; and his commitment, such as it is, is far more easily talked about than acted upon.

It is for this reason that Fowles ends the book with the ambiguous image of the Rembrandt painting. Like the novel, it is a self-portrait with all the paradoxes that entails, a comment on Dan's project and Fowles's own. For Dan, Rembrandt becomes the emblem of his aspiration to whole vision, a new spiritual father. The painting shows Rembrandt as 'the old man in his corner', expressing 'the deepest inner loneliness' and reminding

Dan of something his own father said when he insisted 'that Christ's eyes followed... wherever you went, whatever you did, they watched' (*DM*, pp.667-8), an idea that had terrified Dan. The patriarchal image is contradictory. Rembrandt is a 'formidable sentinel guarding the way back', reminding Dan of what he is attempting to escape. At the same time, the painting reminds him of what he is now attempting to live up to: 'behind the sternness lay the declaration of the one true marriage in the mind mankind is allowed, the ultimate citadel of humanism. No true compassion without will, no true will without compassion.' (*DM*, p.667) Yet despite this confrontation with the ultimate self-awareness of 'those remorseless and aloof Dutch eyes', Dan is already rehearsing how to describe his meeting with Jenny to Jane, 'while she cooked supper for them' (*DM*, p.668), 'knowing she would understand' (*DM*, p.667). It seems that Jane is firmly cast as mother confessor and domestic redeemer in this, the only 'happy' ending Fowles has allowed to be unqualified in his fiction. It is a point which is perhaps meant to reflect more on Dan's manipulations of his own novel, rather than Fowles's.

If the ending of the novel seems too pat, that is possibly symptomatic of the limits imposed by the narrative tactics which Fowles has adopted in order to posit himself as male writer as an element of contradiction, in the manner of Gramsci. The book allows him to explore the impasse facing the middle-aged, middle-class male writer of the 1970s trying to confront his own masculine experience; but one senses Fowles just one step ahead of his character, looking back at him as the character is supposedly looking back at himself, with all the potential slippages and elisions both involve. Dan's self-concern is writ large throughout: it is part of the condition he is struggling to escape but which he nevertheless remains subject to, like an invalid willing away a sickness and insensible to its effects on others. An unease and anxiety lingers behind the composed surface he attempts to establish as surrogate author. It emerges almost inadvertently at the points when he registers the challenge to sexual relations implied by Jane, as when she insists,

'You're romanticizing what I am. Or not understanding what I've become.'
'No man and woman ever fully understand what they've each become. If that condition has to be fufilled, the two sexes ought to be living on different planets. It's an untenable thesis.' (*DM*, p.625)

It might be an untenable thesis for the survival of the race and for the perpetuation of male power, but for the development of women's autonomy many feminists might argue it has a lot to recommend it. What note of revolt Jane sounds, however, is contained and submerged by the wish-fulfilment ending of Dan's novel, indicating the inability and unwillingness of men to step outside the fictions and myths through which they maintain their dominance.

Yet if Fowles leaves us with no overt sense of the possibility for positive change, it is perhaps because such a request would be self-contradictory. The men he depicts are part of the disease he diagnoses. What he puts forward is awareness of the problems as, to use Gramsci's words again, 'a principle of knowledge and therefore action' (*DM*, p.210). Anthony's last advice to Daniel is 'No true change except in ourselves, as we are', which Dan felt to be 'A rarefied idealism, perhaps' (*DM*, p.233). His novel is designed to demonstrate such change in action, precipitated through his relationship with Jane. Fowles's novel, on the other hand, suggests the limits of such change, how it is both provoked and circumscribed by the conditions that produce it. In doing so, he comes the closest so far to a self-examination of the male writer's relation to his own gender identity. He has admitted that he wanted *Daniel Martin* 'to be a personal book',[12] and at the same time he has made it clear that it is not to be taken as unmediated autobiography despite the proximity of experience between himself and his character. He told Mel Gussow that Daniel 'was never conceived of as me',[13] while at the same time admitting 'I don't think I'm hiding so much in this book... In a way, it's a penance.'[14] The penance may have much to do with that guilt generated by feminism, but it is also, one suspects, to do with a personal sense of political commitment. As with Daniel, Fowles has registered outside the novel his own view of his generation as 'sad and failed':[15] 'A lot of my generation gave up creation', he told Gussow when *Daniel Martin* was published in America, 'They became theatre directors, film directors, television media men, Fleet Street men. Very few of the directors have done anything. There was too much grabbing for instantaneous success.'[16] This perhaps argues a limited sense of creative achievement on Fowles's part, as well as his own Calvinistic sense of being one of the elect by having escaped the careerist syndrome—a sense somewhat arrogantly present in his early article 'I write therefore I am'[17] and sitting rather uneasily with his own popularity.

Having said that, *Daniel Martin* is the book in which he comes closest to incorporating the necessity for political change in the challenge to male power, though the structure he adopts avoids the necessity for being prescriptive. He has defined his own politics on a number of occasions as left-wing, though in evasively varying terms. He has described himself as 'a republican', an 'evolutionary socialist',[18] as 'a socialist with an interest in Eurocommunism',[19] but as being deeply pessimistic about governmental politics and the British Labour Party.[20] When James Campbell described him by the 1974 version of the label 'social democrat', which Fowles attributes to himself in *The Aristos*, he replied: 'Yes, I mean I don't hold much brief for Wedgewood Benn or Michael Foot, but there is a feeling that they are trying to get British Socialism, which has gone completely haywire, back on the rails. My view is that capitalism must outgrow itself.' To the question 'Have you ever tried to write an explicitly political book?', Fowles at that point replied 'No. I have no faith in socialist realism. I sincerely hope the Marxism element in this country will grow, but I don't think you can put Marxism across in a novel.'[21] It is, as Gussow suggests, 'a question of politics as well as art' and he quotes Fowles as saying 'I think I offend the right wing' as much with regard to his public reception as his material.[22] In *Daniel Martin* the relationship between politics and art manifests itself in Fowles's choice to abandon the realms of fantasy for a more Lukácsian model of the novel, to assert the novel as what he calls 'a humanistic enterprise'.[23] He told Halpern in 1971, 'I don't like artists who are high on craft and low on humanity. That's one reason I am getting tired of fables',[24] a self-criticism as much as anything else. Perhaps the exorcism involved in writing this book helps explain the relapse, not to say drastic regression, which characterises his most recent production, *Mantissa*.

6

Men, will they ever grow up?:
Mantissa

When Erato, the Muse in *Mantissa*, admits to having written the *Odyssey*, she points out that its original title was '*Men, Will They Ever Grow Up?*. Or just *Men*, for short... It wasn't perfect, by any means. I realize now I never made my basic message clear enough. I rather over-estimated my readers' intelligence, I'm afraid. Half of them still haven't grasped what it's about. Even today.' (*Mt*, p.169) On the basis of *Mantissa*, the answer to her title's question would be 'no', as the book itself points out when she chastises Miles Green, Fowles's surrogate author, for his present production, i.e. *Mantissa*: 'its pathetic. The world's full of highly pertinent male-female situations whose fictional exploration does subtend a viable sociological function—and yet this is the best you can come up with. Muses... I mean, Christ. It's so embarrassing.' (*Mt*, p.88) The ironic self-deprecation of this, jargon and all, strikes a note which is less than confident. His most blatant exposure of male obsessions, *Mantissa* shows all too clearly the limits of Fowles's subversion of male mythologies. In a book which, as David Lodge says, 'sounds like something from the pages of Penthouse' when summarised[1] and which, to adopt a typically weak pun, uses every trick in the book to make its playfulness apparent, it is difficult to avoid feeling that Fowles is merely joking and that the best joke of all would be to be taken seriously. Yet most jokes about sex are by men, for men, and at the expense of women; and in that respect, jokes themselves as Freud has shown *are* serious.[2] The extreme self-parody suggests an accompanying extreme of defensiveness over this most touchy area of male power. Flirtatiously, *Mantissa* offers a choice as to whether we consider it a text of subversive erotic play *à la* Barthes or a text of phallic reinforcement. We may well

147

conclude that, given the present social order, they are the same thing, at least in male hands.

Sarah Benton reports Fowles as agreeing with his wife Elizabeth that 'he should never have published it', explaining that 'he was being bullied by his publishers at the time'.[3] Yet the notion of a direct confrontation with his 'muses' as the sources of his inspiration is one he has had in mind for a number of years. He told Daniel Halpern in 1971: 'I *do* believe in inspiration. I almost believe in muses. In fact, I wrote a short story last year that did bring the muses into modern life. It's very mysterious where good ideas suddenly appear from... I simply wait till the muses come.' When Halpern asked whether this waiting bothered him, Fowles replied chauvinistically, 'No. Women have to be waited for.'[4] Whether this story was the origin or not, the book appears to have been on Fowles's prolific private production line for some time. Donald Hall reported in 1982 that it was begun several years previously and that Fowles had said 'I have often thought that I would like to bring the muse into the twentieth century.'[5] The 'muse', of course, is Fowles's archetypal lost mother or female 'principle' which, in *Mantissa*, appears at its most blatantly Jungian, an anima whose function as Jung imagined it is partly to create animosity, to perversely trick and exasperate the male.[6] As Fowles told Donald Hall, 'In *Mantissa* this *all* comes out in the open. The author and the muse, in that book, are deceiving each other all the time.'[7] The problem, as with Jung's own eccentric formulations, is that this proposes a fixed dualism in human psychology, which transcends history and the social process. If *Daniel Martin* shows something of the Marxist in Fowles, *Mantissa* shows the archetypalist who believes in the 'intrinsic oppositeness of man and woman'.[8]

Of course, it is parody, self-inflicted as much as anything else, and for Fowles the function of the book seems essentially to have been 'comic', though when he was revising it 'frivolous' was the reaction he anticipated. 'I regard one's relation with one's inspiration as fundamentally *comic*' he told Donald Hall,[9] a comment whose oddness again perhaps relates to the defensive unease that can be sensed in the book itself. To Sarah Benton, Fowles explained that Erato was 'meant to be a demon', a point he qualified by saying 'as a writer, when one creates monsters, it is hard not to fall in love with them a little.' Benton's own response to the various personae Erato adopts is that 'None of them is attractive to a feminist, from the punk-like harridan who abuses the man in slabs of hackneyed reproach to the nymphette who finds an unexpected pleasure in being raped by a satyr.'[10]

It is in such a response that we can locate the sources of Fowles's defensiveness perhaps, his guilt that although a fellow-traveller with feminism he still remains subject like all men to the social and psychological paraphernalia of male sexual fantasies; and a fear that, particularly over sex, he will be, as he feels *Mantissa* has been, 'deeply misunderstood'. As Sarah Benton puts it, 'If, in *Mantissa*, one reads "crude" meanings into his chosen sexual imagery of myth, the struggle between the male and female principles, he is not going to defend himself.'[11]

After all the arguments for his exposure of male mythologies, this may seem, and is, something of an abdication of responsibility; but the problem of dealing with sexual fantasy directly is not unexpected. In one sense, all Fowles's fiction is 'sexual fiction', to use a recent though uncritical term.[12] In an interview in May 1970, Fowles commented 'My imagination is highly erotic... I think about almost everything in terms of erotic situations.'[13] We have already seen the contradictions involved in gauging whether his writing analyses the 'erotic' while indulging it; but *Mantissa* raises these problems in a more direct way. Fowles anticipated them when recalling to Stolley that, at the time of the genesis of *The French Lieutenant's Woman*, he was in the middle of a subsequently abandoned novel 'about European attitudes towards nature and conservation, cast in the form of what he calls "a sexual orgy set on a Mediterranean coast"'. He commented: 'I wanted to show that there is something repulsive in mechanically done and described sexual variations. But like any truly erotic person, I had come to regard the publication of explicit sex with great suspicion. It destroys the mystery of it, the pleasure. So I was stuck. I'd fallen into my own trap and I couldn't quite see a way through it.'[14] This suggests that analysing the failures of contemporary sexuality led him into the 'trap' of portraying them *too* convincingly and being unable to escape merely depicting an orgy of sexual variations *per se*. It raises the general question of whether explicitly sexual fiction can be used critically or not. It is an argument we have been continually negotiating in different ways, but with *Mantissa* it becomes more overt in that Fowles is clearly flirting with pornography as a means of exposing the male sexual imagination at its roots.

Fowles suggested to Sarah Benton that the book is 'a metaphor for the growth of language... a small, and private, intervention in the debate about language and literature'.[15] The references to post-structuralist theory in the text are self-evident, but central to *Mantissa*'s effect is that it not only uses the repertoire of sexual writing; it also exploits links *between* sexuality and writing. Crucially, it shows how men construct fantasies of women and obtain power through language, forms of discourse, systems of representation. In doing so, it comes close to the recent arguments, like those put by Angela Carter and Susan Sontag, for some pornography as 'deeply subversive'.[16] In Angela Carter's view, if pornography acquires techniques which, instead of consoling the reader with the 'fiction *of* sex',[17] confront him—the pronoun being specifically male—with the 'anguish of actuality', then he will be faced with a critical split between sexual fantasy and the complexities of actual experiences, 'a dilemma; to opt for the world or to opt for the wet dream?' Out of this dilemma, Carter suggests, 'the moral pornographer might be born'.[18]

The 'might' here is crucial, for Carter's whole argument is really a thesis for testing, and it has been challenged head-on by a number of feminists who in different ways put the case for seeing pornography as the paradigm of male sexuality, male violence against women and a vehicle for maintaining male power. Inevitably, this disallows any attempt to see pornography as subversive and it is a debate which is still being keenly argued.[19] Notably, both Carter and Sontag locate the potential for subverting the social 'fictions' and myths of sexuality in the writing of de Sade and Bataille, both writers who produce work which is self-exposing in the way it lays bare how language manipulates fantasy and image. It is an approach put with eminent clarity by Beverley Brown in her article 'A feminist interest in pornography: some modest proposals'. She argues that pornography is best considered not as a certain kind of explicitness in terms of content, but as a scenario of strategies designed to trigger male sexual fantasies. These exist within a wider spectrum of representations, most notably the representation of women to men and men to themselves in relation to women. Such general representations, advertising and so on, are part of the social power of men over women and pornography is part of that process, with its own repertoire. Beverley Brown suggests that pornography is 'both more specific and less important' than feminists who see it as 'an exemplary moment of patriarchy' might think.[20] She focuses on the genre as one form of representation, a way of constructing images of sexuality and hence definitions of sexuality: 'What makes pornography recognisable are its *non*-transparent features, the elements which constitute it as a distinctive representational genre—a certain rhetoric of the body, forms of narration, placing and wording of captions and titles, stylisations and postures, a repertoire of milieux and costume, lighting techniques etc.'[21]

Beverley Brown's arguments are too subtle to do full justice to in a brief summary like this, but they do provide a starting point for seeing pornographic writing *as* writing, the verbalisation of sex and the construction of fantasy. It is a 'discourse' and to employ that discourse, the repertoire of pornography, in order to expose its own sexual stereotyping in action is, to say the least, a highly contradictory project for the male writer. Susan Sontag suggests that 'pornography isn't a form that can parody itself', since it is already structured as a theatre of stereotypes preferring the ready-made limits of its own self-satisfied routines.[22] If this is the case, then any attempt, however self-aware, to utilise the familiar strategies of pornography subversively will inevitably fall into the trap Fowles himself divined in his abandoned novel. The 'moral pornographer' may be identical with the vicarious pornographer except in the pretence of exposing the very thing he indulges. Both are notably dependent upon the response of their *consumer* for the final measure of their function and this is delineated in a social context within which women are in general subject to the manipulations of male power, a context impossible to step outside.

Yet it is this arena with all its thorny arguments that Fowles enters in *Mantissa* with a self-awareness which is both self-critical and thoroughly self-indulgent, an added *frisson* to the titillations exposed in his book. Miles Green is quite patently a self-parody, an erotically obsessed fantasist for whom writing is sublimated sex, and sex itself a fiction. Green is shown trapped within his own text, an anxious and incompetent novelist caught in the limits of his own sexual fantasies, endlessly revising them for the pure indulgence of going through their possible permutations. What happens in the book is number twenty-nine of an endless series of 'variations' (*Mt*, p.162) through which Green manipulates his fantasy idea of the ideal woman and is himself manipulated by it. The situation reiterates in parody form the whole Fowles repertoire in miniature, and quite self-consciously. It is *The Collector* revisited with Erato accusing Green of being himself, as male novelist, a necrophiliac collector 'of a series of wretched imaginary women' (*Mt*, p.94): 'You just collect and mummify them. Lock them up in a cellar and gloat over them, like Bluebeard.' (*Mt*, p.95) All the elements of Fowles's sexual imagination that we might anticipate are there: the *ménage à trois*; the man subjected to two powerful women; the room cut off from the rest of the world; the archetypal enigmatic female encountering the uncertain male. At the end of the book, Green is already planning his 'next revision' (*Mt*, p.180), mentally rehearsing the possible ways in which he might use the images of his ideal woman and, in the process, revealing how that very activity relates to a notion of male power:

Polynesian, Irish, Venezuelan, Lebanese, Balinese, Indian, Italian, Russian and various points between; shy, passionate, pert, cool; dressed and undressed, tamed and wild, chased and chasing; teasing, in tears, toying, tempestuous... a whole United Nations of female eyes, mouths, breasts, legs, arms, loins, bottoms prettily slink and kaleidoscopically tumble through, or past, the windows of his mind; but, alas, like the images in the fluttered pages of some magazine; or like snowflakes, frozen because unrealizable.

The maddening thing, of course, is that they all lie, waiting to spring or be sprung into charming life and labile reality, inside the body his right arm loosely holds—that is, if the wretched girl (Homer indeed) and her absurdly capricious and banal female vanity... can only be brought to appropriate heel. (*Mt*, pp.181-2)

Erato is the creature of Green's imagination and the book exposes how women are constructed as sexual according to male demands through language. Language as the 'symbolic order' makes women subject to, and the subject of, the phallic text—all very, and appropriately, Lacanian.[23] The activity of 'male *écriture* subduing female flesh to its pleasures', to use Terry Eagleton's formulation,[24] is, as Erato tells Green, 'so crudely repetitive one has to be its victim for only a few pages to guess how it will always work' (*Mt*, p.86). Flann O'Brien's cuckoo clock haunts *Mantissa* as the last word on the absurdities of male sexual pretensions, a 'frantic' wind-up penis which can do nothing but 'cuckoo repeatedly' (*Mt*, p.191).[25] Green's psychic mechanism suffers from a condition Fowles has diagnosed elsewhere as 'nympholepsy. . . a state of rapture inspired by nymphs, hence an ecstasy or frenzy caused by desire of the unattainable',[26] and it is a disease with which 'insecurity-prone men' are 'befuddling' themselves.[27]

All of which might suggest that *Mantissa* is Fowles's final attempt to clear his own head; but, as the arguments about pornography indicate, it is difficult to separate the exposure of sexual fantasy from the indulgence of it. This is particularly a problem since the very self-consciousness of the book constantly calls attention to the fantasy activity of language itself. This double-bind, familiar from the other fiction, is all the more acute given the kinds of fantasy explored in *Mantissa*: if the novelist is, as Green suggests, a repressed 'peeping tom and a flasher' (*Mt*, p.142), then his text is an exhibitionist, with the result that the very act of self-investigation becomes a suspect one and the self-castigation a form of masochism. If this sounds tortuous, it is because Fowles's imagination is at its most devious here, and we can see the paradoxes involved in that readily enough.

Green's situation in the first part of the book is presented as that of a male amnesiac suffering from a 'power cut' (*Mt*, p.12), an identity crisis. The only way he can be 'switched on' is through sex therapy: if he resists treatment, Dr Delfie tells him, 'we shall be forced to employ perverted practices. . . so called' (*Mt*, p.30). Part of his problem, as male and novelist, is a lapse in his 'basic sense of reality' (*Mt*, p.19): he is 'over-attached to the verbalization of feeling, instead of to the direct act of feeling itself' (*Mt*, pp.42-3).

Because of this, he fantasises his relations with women: as Erato tells him later, 'the absurdly romantic role you and the neurotic rest of your kind have always attributed to me bears no relation at all to reality' (*Mt*, p.142); 'you are always trying to turn me into something I'm not' (*Mt*, p.177). As with Fowles's other male case studies, the initial scenario allows Green to act 'less as a person than a problem' (*Mt*, p.21), an object for analysis. Part One is imagined as a consolatory fantasy within the overall fantasy being indulged by Green. He is tucked in bed like a baby in a room whose padded walls remind him of 'schoolgirls' breasts' (*Mt*, p.20), with a mysterious woman doctor whose first words to him, after he realises he is in bed naked, are that she has nothing on under her tunic (*Mt*, p.15). As Dr Delfie, Erato has all the classic elements of the Fowlesian female: she is 'distant' (*Mt*, p.10), enigmatic and provides a 'test' (*Mt*, p.18). She is the parody of the female magus teaching the male the limits of masculinity: as she later says, 'I happen to be a female archetype with an archetypally good sense, developed over several millennia, of deeper values... For all your only too palpable faults and inadequacies, I did have some faint hope that you might one day with my help grasp that the very least your selfish, arrogant and monotonously animal sex owes mine for all its past... Cruelties, is a little affection when we ask for it.' (*Mt*, p.139) As she tells Green, 'I'm your mirror, Just for now.' (*Mt*, p.18) The situation brings out overtly the extent to which such idealisations cater for a deeply rooted male sense of superiority: as in Green's therapy, male power is restored and reinforced by ministering to it as the object of attention, and the appropriation of women as figures of fantasy serves exactly that purpose.

In the first part of the book this amounts to Green being forced into the sexual encounter he secretly desires and part of the power game is in that very pretence. 'Your true evolutionary function, as a male, is to introduce your spermatozoa, that is, your genes, into as many wombs as possible', Dr Delfie tells Green, 'I repeat. Run your hands elsewhere.' (*Mt*, p.27) The fantasy Green caters for is based on a model of dominance and submission, 'Rape. The other way round' (*Mt*, p.42) as he calls it; and the general effect is one which panders to male imperatives. So she invites him 'to see and feel my defencelessness. How small and weak I am, compared to you—how rapable, as it were.' (*Mt*, p.42) The sexual power of the doctor and her nurse are played off against passive roles, the 'schoolmistress' (*Mt*, p.30) and the 'demure and obedient niece waiting for a kiss from an uncle' (*Mt*, p.34). They are the classic poses of women imagined by male sexual fantasy, counters played out in Green's imagination, and shown to be such by the absurd manner in which Green conceives his own role. Though 'powerless' to prevent himself being sexually aroused, his 'entire moral being continued to protest at this abject surrender to animality' (*Mt*, p.36) and this leads him to speculate that his lost identity might be that of a guardian of public morality, an MP 'selflessly braving the sex-hells of Hamburg and Copenhagen' in his dedication to his duty: 'No silent Member, he: he would catch Mr Speaker's eye and rise, nothing could stop him rising, with aplomb and dignity and full force, to his most solemn and convincing height.' (*Mt*, p.38-9) It is a ludicrous Lord Longford spoof whose silliness, like the whole hospital scenario, is, one has to assume, indicative of Green's sex-befuddled brain and indicted as such by Erato's explosive entry in the second part.

The ostensible aim of *Mantissa*, then, is to lay bare its own fantasising in action. Erato bursts in as an avenging female 'Nemesis' (*Mt*, p.52) castigating Green as a 'fuckin' chauvinist pig' (*Mt*, p.53), 'a typical capitalist sexist parasite' (*Mt*, p.55), who aims at 'degradin' women by turnin' us into one-dimensional sex-objects' (*Mt*, p.58): 'Givin' that cardboard cut-out *my* face, *my* body' (*Mt*, p.55). She is 'a victim of the historical male-fascist conspiracy' (*Mt*, p.54) and tells him 'You don't kid a sister.' (*Mt*, p.55) Green's reaction is 'half dubious, half imploring. "Don't say you've gone political."' (*Mt*, p.54) The tone of this is indicative: as Erato says, 'Look. Ever since I got into serious liberation, you've been takin' the mickey. I got your number, mate. You're the original pig. Numero Uno.' (*Mt*, p.56) This, with its echoes of the numerous similar castigations of male 'heroes' by angry women in the other books, is the key to the defensive note in *Mantissa*. It is plain that this feminist is herself a cardboard cut-out, a parody of radical feminism the result of which allows Green to accuse her of behaving 'just like a man... Instant value-judgements. Violent sexual prejudice. To say nothing of trying to hide behind the roles and language of a milieu to which you do not belong.' (*Mt*, p.55) The self-chastisement in *Mantissa* is clearly the product of guilt but it is equally a manipulative strategy for blunting some of the edge of feminism's attacks. The display of male sexuality as puerile conveniently minimises its social effects, while radical feminism is presented as a throwaway stereotype, literally throwaway since Erato changes her pose, defusing its impact. The result is a crafty realignment which, whilst seeming to allow for the most overt criticism, in fact incorporates it in a reconstituted male mythology.

A key manoeuvre in this wiliness is the focus Fowles puts on language as an activity. The puns and the game-playing emphasise the process of verbalising sexuality in an ambiguous way. At the end of the first part, Green's orgasm is represented by an accelerating speech from Dr Delfie, literally an orgasm of words since what is being produced *is* the text, the verbal mechanism for the fantasist. Green's 'baby' (*Mt*, p.45) is the chapter itself, 'a lovely little story. And you made it all by yourself.' (*Mt*, p.48) The self-enclosed nature of the male sexual imagination is both exposed and confirmed by Fowles's display of the eroticising of language and of the way language constructs a male idea of woman, since it all occurs within a view of sexual activity which does nothing to challenge predominantly male tastes. The language play, while it might seem a self-subverting tactic designed to disrupt and reveal how sexuality is made up by men, also serves to reinforce male assumptions. This is particularly apparent in the way Fowles shows Green making Erato up from words and, in the process, doing the same himself.

From punk feminist, Erato is transformed into her role as Grecian muse, the effect of which she herself points out:

> '...You look stunning. Out of this world.' He seeks for words, or appears to do so. 'More childlike. Vulnerable. Sweet.'
> 'More feminine?'
> 'Incontestably.'
> 'Easier to exploit.'
> 'I didn't mean that at all. Honestly... a dream. Just the sort of girl one would like to take home to meet mother.' (*Mt*, p.59)

As with the laboured puns, the clichés in Green's response are there to show up his stereotyping mind in action and the way language acts to define and contain women within certain roles or imagery. Yet while the book uses Erato to voice such criticisms of the male fantasist's power, she is also increasingly recruited as merely a part of his imagination in action, the castigation having a titillatory function. By calling attention to the effects of language, Erato is turned into the purveyor of verbalised sexuality and her tauntings are part of the process.

As part of their increasing 'badinage' (*Mt*, p.116), she allows Green ten sentences to make 'a full, proper and formal apology' (*Mt*, p.61) for his manipulations of her. The sentences, culminating in a two-and-a-half-page long syntactical *tour de force*, display all the deviousness of the male ego and highlight Green's containment of her verbally. They vary from the idealised 'You've always been my perfect woman' (*Mt*, p.62) to the blatant: 'because you really are (dash) and I am not (underlined) being a male chauvinist (dash) one of the most god-awful cock-teasers in the history of this planet and I sometimes think how much easier the whole damn business would be if we were all gay and if you go on like this we very probably shall be and then where will you be'. (*Mt*, pp.65-6) While Erato counter-attacks critically, she is constantly sexualised as an idea: 'I've never met such arrogance. And the sheer blasphemy! I do *not* inspire pornography. I never have. And as for that other disgusting word... everyone knows that my chief characteristic happens to be a supreme maidenliness—and once and for all will you *stop* looking at my nipples!' (*Mt*, p.66) It is precisely this sexual manipulation of the women figure as the mentor of a recalcitrant male that Fowles shows to be Green's most devious fantasy, a manipulation which takes place through language itself and which reflects back self-critically on Fowles's own writing. While Erato accuses Green of being a mere 'composer of erotica' and having 'typical male pseudo-intellectual's sexist' beliefs (*Mt*, p.70), she is used verbally as the vehicle for sexual ideas. She reminds Green how many other 'sensitive geniuses' (*Mt*, p.70) have had her clothes off; she seems irresistibly drawn, despite her chastisements of him, to look at his penis (*Mt*, pp.69, 72); she goes coy and admits herself 'not totally unaware that you're male and I'm female' (*Mt*, p.68); she allows him to tease with her clothes so that 'the whole top of the garment threatens to fall' (*Mt*, p.69), allows him to stroke her nipples whilst saying 'I don't know why men put such enormous value on it' (*Mt*, p.71), and finally takes her clothes off, standing before him 'like some Victorian artist's model' (*Mt*, p.71).

What is offered here is the *idea* of the defiant woman transformed into a compliant one through language. Most notably, Erato becomes complicit in this herself through her account of her supposed sexual initiation by the Greek satyr Mopsus, who 'had more sex in his little toe-nail than you do in your whole boring body' (*Mt*, p.70). She tells the story ostensibly to put Green in his place and prove 'how inept and ignorant most of you are' (*Mt*, p.70). It is 'a tutorial... about sexual arrogance' and a lesson to the inadequate novelist Green in 'how to get simply and quickly to the point' (*Mt*, p.72); but the function of the recitation is purely voyeuristic, a fantasy-correlative for Green's accompanying physical encroachment upon her body. The story-telling is framed for male ears: since it is part of the male novelist's imaginings, its accuracy is irrelevant as shown by the way Erato's age dwindles from being sixteen to being a defenceless eleven-year-old at the climax. What she recites is a rape, done in such a way as to assume the predominant male viewpoint on rape and sexuality in general—that women inevitably want sex when men do, in ways which suit men, even if they deny it. More specifically, the language invites the hearer to conjure up the scene for himself:

'... when I'd finished oiling myself I lay on my tummy, in the innocent way schoolgirls do.' Her eyes survey his. 'If you can picture that. How defenceless I was, how exposed.' (*Mt*, p.79)

'... to my horror I felt the intruder's hairy body and... something else lower itself on my innocent twelve-year-old olive-oiled bottom.' There is a silence. 'Oh honestly. Do you have *always* to be so literal-minded?'
  He kissed the nape of her neck.
  'I wanted to scream, to struggle. But I knew it would be in vain. It was either surrender to his lust or be murdered. Actually he wasn't violent at all. He did bite my neck, but only in play. Then he started to whisper things. Wicked things, but I forced myself to listen...' A few moments later she resumes, staring up into his eyes. 'I was beyond resisting by then. Mere wax

in his hands. I could only stare up into his lascivious, lecherous eyes. If you
can imagine that.'
    He smiles down into her dark ones, and nods. (*Mt*, p.80)

We are made aware of the construction of this as a fantasy, a
process whereby language makes Erato available to the
penetration of the male imagination and one which is mutually
acknowledged in a verbal equivalent of the 'look' which John Ellis
and Paul Willeman[28] describe as one strategy in visual
pornography. The ambiguity is that whilst Fowles rehearses this
scenario with practised competence his text calls immediate
attention to its own activity. 'You're like all pornographers',
Erato immediately informs Green after the end of her tale, 'As
soon as it's a question of his lordship's pleasure, reality flies out of
the window.' (*Mt*, p.81) All his fantasies, she tells him, involve not
one but '*two* entirely mythical beings', the male's view of himself as
sexually potent satyr and his view of the woman as an instrument
for gratification. The modern satyr is 'someone who invents a
woman on paper so that he can force her to say and do things no
real woman in her right mind ever would', and she ends her
castigation, 'I'm just one more miserable fantasy figure your
diseased mind is trying to conjure up out of nothing.' (*Mt*, p.85)
    In this manner, *Mantissa* labours within a solipsistic critique of
its own activity, inescapably caught in a circular process of self-
indictment and self-gratification, an evidently trivial text as its
title indicates but whose very triviality attempts to say something
serious about its subject—the male sexual imagination. The
weaknesses of the book, its frenetic self-awareness, its laborious
puns, are all attempts at self-characterisation of that subject. As a
writer, Erato tells Green, 'you have always had such a rare talent
for not being able to express yourself' (*Mt*, p.167), but the
precariousness of this anti-art strategy lies in the limits imposed by
its own imaginative exhaustion. It makes the point all too
blatantly that Green is trapped within those textual limits, the
purveyor and subject of his own imaginings, 'locked in the same
prison cell' (*Mt*, p.128) as his fantasies. As Erato tells him, 'you
can't walk out of your own brain' (*Mt*, p.123).
    This approach allows Fowles to indulge the use of fictionality to

expose role-playing to the full in the battle between author and character over who controls whom. At the mercy of his own ideology, Green's male self is a fiction too, a male 'I' made up within a system of language in the first pages of his text. Initially, he is an 'it' floating undefined among 'associated morphs and phonemes, [which] returned like the algebraic formulae of schooldays, lodged in the mind by ancient rote... It was conscious, evidently; but bereft of pronoun, all that distinguishes person from person.' (*Mt*, p.9) His awareness becomes placed when he sees two women and realises 'it was a centre of attention, an I of sorts... not just an I, but a male I. That must be where the inrushing sense of belowness, impotence, foolishness came from.' (*Mt*, p.10) Green's sense of insecurity about his own role as a character relates specifically to his male identity, what Erato calls 'his exceedingly dubious status. I wonder who's pulling *his* strings?' (*Mt*, p.87) Fowles gets the sense of the male as the creator of a dominant discourse and as the victim himself of its 'rules' (*Mt*, p.89) and restrictions. Erato's demand that he consider 'what a horror it would be' for men to have to do what women are forced to do within the patriarchal system is a central indictment: 'to have to occupy a role and function that escapes all normal biological laws. All on her own. No outside help, never a day off. Constantly having to dress up as this, dress up as that. The impossible boredom of it. The monotony. The schizophrenia. Day after day of being mauled about in people's minds, misunderstood, travestied, degraded.' (*Mt*, pp.92-3) At the same time, men subject themselves to a similar imprisonment in pursuit of their own power; and to push the point home, Fowles has Erato invent *her* imaginary version of their relationship, her own manipulation of Green within his. She envisages him as a businessman, to his disgust a successful banana importer, a 'perfectly nice man in his way. Just a little... limited and deformed by his milieu and profession.' (*Mt*, p.104) She writes him into the role of married man, arranging their first liaison in the banana ripening shed against a background of 'thousands of detumescent vegetable penises' (*Mt*, p.109) and, as the final indignity in Green's eyes, she makes him turn gay after losing her.

The apparent nakedness of the male novelist's fantasies is itself made a joke: when Green tells Erato 'I've got nothing on', her reply is 'Great. Now the whole friggin' world can see you for what you really are.' (*Mt*, p.56) The self-deflating humour is a strategy of evasion in a book which, as Fowles's subsequent uncertainty about it suggests, he must have felt comes very close to mere indulgence. Its uncertainties extend through the humour to issues which he himself has seen as crucial. Erato's suggestion that there might be 'some new sort of meeting' (*Mt*, p.67) between them 'outside the illusions of the text' (*Mt*, p.107) indicates a desire for the realignment of male-female relations; but Green's bruised ego allows for no feasible escape: he asserts

> You may take my clothes away, you may stop me leaving. You cannot change my feelings.'
> 'I know. You silly thing.'
> 'Then this is a ridiculous waste of time.'
> 'Unless you change them yourself.'
> 'Never.' (*Mt*, p.124)

His self-enclosed stasis is revealed as the condition of his power in the long, misogynistical soliloquy which accompanies the final 'charming picture of sexual concord; clinging female, protective male'. Fowles ironically invites indulgence for his reactionary 'hero'—'All male sympathies must go to Miles Green; or so Miles Green himself overwhelmingly feels' (*Mt*, p.181)—while the monologue reproduces some of the central anxieties he has himself identified in men's response to women in contemporary society. Green is ready to allow a degree of autonomy, 'but not over what women owe men in the most fundamental thing of all. There must be a point, in that area, where the teasing and joking has to stop, and biological reality, why women are here in the first place, given its due.' (*Mt*, p.184) Green's tirade is transparently defensive chauvinism at its most blatant and pernicious, a point reinforced by his final fantasy. Having transformed Erato into a Japanese geisha girl, his 'infinitely compliant woman, true wax at last' (*Mt*, p.186), he finds himself turned into a literal hairy satyr and, leaping on the bed with 'the primeval cry of the male' (*Mt*, p.190), he knocks himself out to the sound of the frantic cuckooing of the clock. The book ends reiterating its own opening paragraph, as another variation gets under way, this time with

Nurse Cory ready to give 'the initial treatment' (*Mt*, p.172).

A suitably absurd ending to an absurd book, one which Fowles evidently would not want taking too seriously, it is all the more revealing for that reason. The politics of the sex-gender debate are totally subsumed by the throwaway humour, the devious self-criticism and the ambiguous awareness of the sexualising of language. Perhaps any attempt to use sexual fantasy critically will lead a male writer into an overt concern with its operations in a way which reiterates them as well as exposing them. Like his surrogate, Fowles himself is the victim of his own archetypes with their insistent polarities: 'if we reject woman as fertile mother and as mystic virgin, then we are (or appear to be) left only with woman as source of pleasure, as an instrument, as a substitute for masturbation—in short, as a houri'.[29] As usual, the qualification leaves Fowles an escape route and, again as usual, it is not too convincing. *Mantissa* is his attempt to go through the looking-glass only to be caught behind it and for quite transparent reasons.

In the section of her book on male violence against women in which she considers pornography, Elizabeth Wilson has put the following view:

> I do not myself believe that pornography 'speaks' male power in the some simple way. It seems rather to reveal the disintegration of male sexuality under the pressures of a commoditizing, fetishizing culture. Far from being the celebration of male power, pornography sometimes seems designed to reassure men and allay fear of impotence; where it is violent and sadistic it displays fear and loathing not only of women but also of male passivity.[30]

This crucial link between male power and male anxiety or fear is the contradiction at the centre of the male mythologies that Fowles engages with so ambiguously, and not least in *Mantissa*. Against Erato's accusations, Miles Green defends his fantasies in true male liberal intellectual fashion: 'The sex was just a metaphor, for heaven's sake' (*Mt*, p.115), but as with jokes, where sexual power is involved, such excuses are devious evasions. It is there, in the question of power, that the 'difference' between men and women adheres, and in this sense fantasy and fiction have their part to play in either bolstering or dismantling the myths of power. Male desire and female desire, male fantasies and female fantasies, may not in fact be specific to each sex as such. What *is* specific is the relative positions of power from which they operate. In a recent essay exploring this issue, Wendy Holloway puts it like this: 'The way that vulnerability is a product of desire for the Other may well be the same for women and men, but the positions that can be taken up in order to resist the Other's power must be different because of gender. It is for this reason that men's and women's power in sexual relationships cannot be said to be equivalent. It is not a question of "equal but different".'[31] She goes on to argue positively that 'It is not impossible to change these dynamics', but points out that men will have to do 'some hard work on those feelings' if they are to demystify their dominant view of women and themselves.[32] The key to this in terms of ideology lies in part with the notion of woman as Other, the resolution to male doubt and, concomitantly, the victims of male power. It is perhaps this which, more than anything, is responsible in lived personal terms for the psychological need in men to perpetuate a power relation to women—the myth of the woman as Other, as the rationale for male identity, as the demarcation of male identity, that which is denied in order to define the male in the first instance, that which is desired in order to guarantee and maintain the definition. This legacy of the social construction of masculinity is continually reconstructed in the images men make of women, images which are conversely images of men themselves, speaking the contradictory dialectic of male dependency on women and the concurrent male imposition of control upon women. To dismantle this ideology, as Elizabeth Wilson says, 'first we have to understand the fears behind the fantasies, the substitution of omnipotence for impotence, the projection into women of male fear. It is not that women are passive. They represent *male* passivity and that is what has to be destroyed, over and over again, and with compulsive monotony—created with the gags and hoods and the bondage, and then fragmented with the power of the prick. But this anxious reassuring ritual never does allay the fear for long.'[33]

By virtue of its very contradictions, Fowles's work has a great deal to say about this relationship between power, anxiety and fantasy. Not least, it demonstrates that it is not enough merely to reverse the mythology and have the deposed knight rescued by the fair damosel. If these myths of ideology are to be demystified men themselves must be prepared to confront the dragons of their own captivity. Only then will an honest engagement with feminism and a positive contribution to the dismantling of male power be possible.

Notes

Chapter 1: John Fowles and the masculinity myth.

1. S. Allen (et al.), *Conditions of Illusion: Papers from the Women's Movement* (Leeds: Feminist Books, 1974), p.109.
2. John Fowles, *Daniel Martin* (St Albans: Triad/Panther, 1978), p.7. All further references to John Fowles's book-length works are given in abbreviated form as in the Preface.
3. I owe the formulation of this point to Beatrix Campbell in a discussion which she led at Hull University in 1982. See A. Coote and B. Campbell, *Sweet Freedom: The Struggle for Women's Liberation* (London: Pan, 1982), p.240.
4. A. Tolson, *The Limits of Masculinity* (London: Tavistock, 1977), pp.13, 51.
5. *ibid.* p.24.
6. *ibid.* p.25.
7. Jeffrey Weeks, *Sex, Politics and Society* (London: Longmans, 1981), p.7.
8. S. Benton, 'Adam and Eve' in *New Socialist*, 11 (May–June 1983), p.19.
9. *ibid.* p.19.
10. D. Hall, 'John Fowles's garden' in *Esquire*, 98 (October 1982), p.96.
11. R. Boston, 'John Fowles, alone but not lonely' in *New York Times Book Review* (9 November 1969), p.2.
12. R. Huffaker, *John Fowles* (Boston, Mass.: G.K. Hall, 1980), p.22.
13. S. Benton, 'Adam and Eve' in *New Socialist*, 11 (May–June 1983), p.18.
14. R.K. Singh, 'An encounter with John Fowles' in *Journal of Modern Literature* 8, 2 (1980), p.195.
15. J. Campbell, 'An interview with John Fowles' in *Contemporary Literature*, 17, 4 (1976), p.467.
16. R. Boston, 'John Fowles, alone but not lonely' in *New York Times Book Review* (9 November 1969), p.2.
17. J. Campbell, 'An interview with John Fowles' in *Contemporary Literature*, 17, 4 (1976), p.467.
18. S. Benton, 'Adam and Eve' in *New Socialist*, 11 (May–June 1983), p.18.
19. *ibid.* p.19.

20. P. Conradi, *John Fowles* (London: Methuen, 1982), p.91.
21. John Fowles, 'Notes on an unfinished novel' in *The Novel Today*, ed. M. Bradbury, (London: Fontana, 1982), p.146.
22. J. Campbell, 'An interview with John Fowles' in *Contemporary Literature*, 17, 4 (1976), p.465.
23. For some information on the Zen influences on Fowles see R. Huffaker, *John Fowles* (Boston, Mass.: G.K. Hall, 1980), p.17, where Huffaker quotes a letter from Fowles about his reading of Alan Watt's *The Way of Zen* during the 1950s. See also Fowles's essay, 'Seeing nature whole' in *Harper's Magazine*, 259 (November 1979), pp.49-68.
24. A. Carter, *The Sadeian Woman* (London, Virago, 1979), p.5.
25. E. Trudgill, *Madonnas and Magdalens* (New York: Holmes and Meier, 1976), p.28.
26. R.K. Singh, 'An encounter with John Fowles' in *Journal of Modern Literature*, 8, 2 (1980), pp.189-90.
27. S. Benton, 'Adam and Eve' in *New Socialist*, 11 (May–June 1983), p.18.
28. *ibid.* p.19.
29. N. Frye, *The Secular Scripture* (Cambridge, Mass.: Harvard, 1976), p.104.
30. R. Huffaker, *John Fowles* (Boston, Mass.: G.K. Hall, 1980), p.26.
31. L. Sage, 'John Fowles' in *The New Review*, (1 October 1974), p.37.
32. R. Huffaker, *John Fowles* (Boston, Mass.: G.K. Hall, 1980), p.117.
33. *ibid.* pp.24-5.
34. E. Reynaud, *Holy Virility: The Social Construction of Masculinity* (London: Pluto, 1983), p.77.
35. S. Heath, *The Sexual Fix* (London: Macmillan, 1982), p.126.
36. *ibid.* p.89.
37. M. Bragg, 'Interview with John Fowles' from 'The South Bank Show' London Weekend Television, transcript P/NO 80103, 1982, p.3.
38. In his interview with Raman Singh, Fowles describes an 'assistant professor of psychiatry at Harvard [who] wrote a very interesting article about *The French Lieutenant's Woman*. He treated it as a patient and analyzed the book. I don't go all the way with his analysis, but I go totally with his theory that novelists are genetically made; and then by circumstances over which you have no control in the first few years of your life.' He later returns to the topic of Rose's essay and says that all writing 'is therapy, isn't it? All writers must have a tremendous fix; they're obsessive. This is what's so marvellous about this psychiatrist's... analysis of why people write. Why is it that you're never satisfied? Why do you go on trying, trying, trying again? Obviously what you're trying to do is—this is my theory—trying to achieve some primal state of perfection and total happiness, which you're doomed never to experience because you'll never be one year old again... You're doomed to be on an eternal hunt.' See R.K. Singh, 'An encounter with John Fowles' in *Journal of Modern Literature*, 8, 2 (1980), pp.184-5 and pp.199-200.
39. G. Rose, '*The French Lieutenant's Woman*: The unconscious significance of a novel to its author' in *American Imago*, 29 (Summer 1972), p.173.

40. *ibid.* pp.169-70.
41. John Fowles, 'Hardy and the Hag' in *Thomas Hardy After Fifty Years*, ed. L. St John Butler, (London: Macmillan, 1977), p.31.
42. *ibid.* p.31.
43. *ibid.* p.41.
44. *ibid.* p.28.
45. *ibid.* p.29.
46. *ibid.* p.33.
47. L. Sage, 'John Fowles' in *The New Review* (1 October 1974), p.35.
48. John Fowles, 'Hardy and the Hag' in *Thomas Hardy After Fifty Years*, ed. L. St John Butler, (London: Macmillan, 1977), pp.37-8.
49. *ibid.* p.35.
50. *ibid.* p.40.
51. *ibid,* p.36.
52. *ibid.* p.40.
53. D. Halpern, 'A sort of exile in Lyme Regis' in *London Magazine* (10 March 1971), p.36.
54. Barry Olshen, for example, says that Fowles 'was an avowed feminist before it was fashionable to be so, and some of his non-fiction pieces illustrate with equal clarity his concern for the harmonious relations between the sexes', which, in addition to its unquestioning assumption that a man can be called a feminist, seems to imply that the feminist project is aimed at achieving 'harmonious relations between the sexes', which is to miss its political edge altogether. See B. Olshen, *John Fowles* (New York: Ungar, 1978), p.14. More questionable still is the approach taken by Peter Wolfe, who not only seems unquestioningly to accept Fowles's views of the female principle but also puts his own view that 'women's greater capacity for faith and imagination' is 'explainable biologically'. See P. Wolfe, *John Fowles, Magus and Moralist* (London: Associated University Press, 1979), p.40. Even Peter Conradi, though he comments on Fowles's 'oddly complacent' feminism as we have seen, tends to leave that allegiance and Fowles's notion of the feminine principle unproblematic; and he goes so far as implicitly to endorse Fowles's anxiety over radical feminism in this quotation from the Singh interview: '"It always worries me when I see the feminine principle itself being attacked by women," he has understandably said.' See P. Conradi, *John Fowles* (London: Methuen, 1982), p.91.
55. C. Hieatt, '*Eliduc* revisited: John Fowles and Marie de France' in *English Studies in Canada*, 3 (Fall 1977), p.357.
56. J. Culler, *On Deconstruction* (London: Routledge and Kegan Paul, 1983), p.55.
57. M. Bragg, 'Interview with John Fowles' from 'The South Bank Show' London Weekend Television, transcript P/NO 80103, 1982, p.6.
58. B. Olshen and T. Olshen, *John Fowles: A Reference Guide* (Boston, Mass.: G.K. Hall, 1980), p.viii.
59. L. Sage, 'John Fowles' in *The New Review*, (1 October 1974), p.35.

Chapter 2: Bluebeard and the voyeurs.

1. J. Campbell, 'An interview with John Fowles' in *Contemporary Literature*, 17, 4 (1976), p.457.
2. R. Newquist, 'John Fowles' in *Counterpoint* ed R. Newquist, (Chicago, Ill.: Rand McNally, 1964), p.219.
3. M. Bragg, 'Interview with John Fowles' from 'The South Bank Show' London Weekend Television, transcript P/NO 80103, 1982: 'I think I know that aspect of Freud quite well. I can't think of any clear case of one saying, well this couldn't have happened. It's simply because of the way it's described of course. It's essentially in fictional narrative terms although they were true cases.'
4. See Phyllis Chesler, *About Men* (The Women's Press, 1978); Andrea Dworkin, *Pornography: Men Possessing Women* (The Women's Press, 1981), chapter 2; Paul Hoch, *White Hero Black Beast: Racism, Sexism and the Mask of Masculinity* (London: Pluto, 1979), pp.71, 75.
5. See chapter 5, p.103.
6. Peter Wolfe, *John Fowles, Magus and Moralist* (London: Associated University Press, 1976), p.66.
7. *ibid.* p.72.
8. John Fowles, 'For the dark' in *New Statesman* (18 February 1977), p.222.
9. See Juliet Mitchell and Jacqueline Rose (eds), *Feminine Sexuality: Jacques Lacan and the École Freudienne* (London: Macmillan, 1982), pp.6, 32, 38.
10. Andrea Dworkin, *Pornography: Men Possessing Women* (London: The Women's Press, 1981), p.47.
11. Paul Hoch, *White Hero Black Beast: Racism, Sexism and the Mask of Masculinity* (London: Pluto, 1979), p.74 quotes Malraux to this effect.
12. P. Conradi, *John Fowles* (London: Methuen, 1982), p.34.
13. *ibid.* p.35.
14. B. Olshen, *John Fowles* (New York: Unger, 1978), p.20.
15. *ibid.* p.25.
16. John Fowles, 'Hardy and the Hag' in *Thomas Hardy After Fifty Years* ed L. St John Butler (London: Macmillan, 1977), p.38.
17. R. Boston, 'John Fowles, alone but not lonely' in *New York Times Book Review* (9 November 1969), p.2.
18. Michel Foucault, *The History of Sexuality: An Introduction*, tr. R. Hurley (Harmondsworth: Penguin, 1981), pp.62-3.

Chapter 3: Masculinity on trial.

1. I have chosen to use the original version of *The Magus* as the primary text for this discussion since it allows a sense of the historical shift between

Fowles's views of men in the 1950s and 1960s (when he conceived and wrote the book) and his views in the later novels. The revised version is referred to at points when the changes are of particular interest.

2. B. Olshen, *John Fowles* (New York: Ungar, 1978), p.53.

3. R. Binns, 'A new version of *The Magus*' in *Critical Quarterly*, 19, 4 (1977), p.83.

4. John Fowles, 'The trouble with starlets' in *Holiday*, 39 (June 1966), p.17.

5. J. Campbell, 'An interview with John Fowles' in *Contemporary Literature*, 17, 4 (1976), p.466.

6. *ibid.* p.458. See L. Sage, 'John Fowles' in *The New Review* (1 October 1974), p.33 for the same view.

7. See the summary of Tolson's views given in chapter 5, footnote 5, on p.172.

8. R. Huffaker, *John Fowles* (Boston, Mass.: G.K. Hall, 1980), p.47.

9. D. Halpern, 'A sort of exile in Lyme Regis' in *London Magazine* (10 March 1971), p.46; J. Campbell, 'An interview with John Fowles' in *Contemporary Literature*, 17, 4 (1976), p.463.

10. John Fowles, 'Notes on an unfinished novel' in *The Novel Today*, ed M. Bradbury (London: Fontana, 1982), pp.146-7.

11. R. Singh, 'An encounter with John Fowles' in *Journal of Modern Literature*, 8, 2 (1980), p.197.

12. John Fowles, 'The Falklands and a death foretold' in *The Guardian* (14 August 1982), p.7.

13. L.R.Edwards, 'Changing our imaginations' in *Massachusetts Review*, 11 (Summer 1970), p.607.

14. D. Halpern, 'A sort of exile in Lyme Regis' in *London Magazine* (10 March 1971), p.35.

15. R. Singh, 'An encounter with John Fowles' in *Journal of Modern Literature*, 8, 2 (1980), p.186.

16. *See* A. Tolson, *The Limits of Masculinity* (London: Tavistock, 1977), p.118: 'Men hang on to this institution, not simply for chauvinist motives, or because they do not possess the personal courage to change, but because they cannot foresee a future beyond its determination.'

17. P. Wolfe, *John Fowles, Magus and Moralist* (London: Associated University Press, 1976), p.116.

18. R. Huffaker, *John Fowles* (Boston, Mass.: G.K. Hall, 1980), p.67.

19. D. Halpern, 'A sort of exile in Lyme Regis' in *London Magazine* (10 March 1971), p.35.

20. J. Campbell, 'An interview with John Fowles' in *Contemporary Literature*, 17, 4 (1976), pp.457, 458.

21. John Fowles, 'For the dark' in *New Statesman*, (18 February 1977), p.222.

22. John Fowles, *Poems* (New York: Ecco Press, 1973), p.2.

23. R. Huffaker, *John Fowles* (Boston, Mass.: G.K. Hall, 1980), p.286.

24. *ibid.* p.28.

25. C. Hieatt, '*Eliduc* revisited: John Fowles and Marie de France' in *English*

Studies in Canada, 3 (Fall, 1977), p.354. I have neglected the relevant stories from *The Ebony Tower* for reasons of space, but David Williams's guilty flirtation with imaginary infidelity makes him a slightly more sympathetic study of the same duplicity as Urfe's, while Breasley is a cruder and more overtly patriarchal Conchis.

26. R. Huffaker, *John Fowles* (Boston, Mass.: G.K. Hall, 1980), p.44.
27. R. Robinson, 'Giving the reader a choice—a conversation with John Fowles' in *The Listener* (31 October 1974), p.584.
28. John Fowles, *Poems* (New York: Ecco Press, 1973), pp.viii-ix.

Chapter 4: The figure in the unconscious.

1. M. Bragg, 'Interview with John Fowles' from 'The South Bank Show', London Weekend Television, transcript P/NO 80103, 1982, p.3.
2. *ibid.* p.10.
3. *ibid.* p.7.
4. *ibid.* p.4.
5. John Fowles, 'Notes on an unfinished novel' in *The Novel Today* ed M. Bradbury (London: Fontana, 1982), p.138.
6. E. Trudgill, *Madonnas and Magdalens* (New York: Holmes and Meier, 1976), p.101.
7. B. Harrison, *Separate Spheres* (London: Croom Helm, 1978), pp.97-8.
8. R. Tannahill, *Sex in History* (London: Hamish Hamilton, 1980), p.353.
9. See especially Michel Foucault, *The History of Sexuality: An Introduction* (Harmondsworth: Penguin, 1981), *passim*.
10. F. Harrison, *The Dark Angel: Aspects of Victorian Sexuality* (London: Fontana, 1979), p.8.
11. J. Weeks, *Sex, Politics and Society* (London: Longmans, 1981), p.38.
12. *ibid.* p.39.
13. *ibid.* p.40.
14. R.L. Stevenson, *Dr Jekyll and Mr Hyde* (London: Collins, 1958), p.62.
15. M. Bragg, 'Interview with John Fowles' from 'The South Bank Show', London Weekend Television, transcript P/NO 80103, 1982, p.33.
16. *See* chapter 1, pp.12-14.
17. Z. Fairbairns, *Stand We At Last* (London: Virago, 1983), p.230.
18. John Fowles, 'Notes on an unfinished novel' in *The Novel Today* ed M. Bradbury (London: Fontana, 1982), p.141.
19. John Fowles, 'Hardy and the Hag' in *Thomas Hardy After Fifty Years* ed L. St John Butler (London: Macmillan, 1977), p.28.
20. John Fowles, 'Notes on an unfinished novel' in *The Novel Today* ed M. Bradbury (London: Fontana, 1982), p.142.
21. P. Conradi, *John Fowles* (London: Methuen, 1982), p.67.
22. E. Mansfield, 'A sequence of endings: the manuscripts of *The French Lieutenant's Woman*' in *Journal of Modern Literature*, 8, 2 (1980-1), p.284.

23. S. Benton, 'Adam and Eve' in *New Socialist*, 11 (May-June 1983), p.19.

24. R. Tannahill, *Sex in History* (London: Hamish Hamilton, 1980), p.356, quotes from Leopold Deslandes, *Manhood: The Causes of its Premature Decline with Directions for Perfect Restoration* (1843) to the effect that sex with a prostitute was 'generally attended with less derangement' than sex with a wife.

25. John Fowles, 'Notes on an unfinished novel' in *The Novel Today* ed M. Bradbury (London: Fontana, 1982), pp.140-1.

26. E. Mansfield, A sequence of endings: the manuscripts of *The French Lieutenant's Woman*' in *Journal of Modern Literature*, 8, 2 (1980-1), p.281.

27. M. Bragg, 'Interview with John Fowles' from 'The South Bank Show', London Weekend Television, transcript P/NO 80103, 1982, pp.3, 26.

28. L.R. Edwards, 'Changing our imaginations', *Massachusetts Review*, 11 (Summer 1970), p.607.

29. E. Mansfield, A sequence of endings: the manuscripts of *The French Lieutenant's Woman*' in *Journal of Modern Literature*, 8, 2 (1980-1), p.281.

30. John Fowles, 'Notes on an unfinished novel' in *The Novel Today* ed M. Bradbury (London: Fontana, 1982), p.147.

31. M. Bragg, 'Interview with John Fowles' from 'The South Bank Show', London Weekend Television, transcript P/NO 80103, 1982, p.16.

32. *See* chapter 1, pp.20-3.

33. P. Wolfe, *John Fowles, Magus and Moralist* (London: Associated University Press, 1976), p.153.

34. F. Harrison, *The Dark Angel: Aspects of Victorian Sexuality* (London: Fontana, 1979), pp.31-2.

35. R. Tannahill, *Sex in History* (London: Hamish Hamilton, 1980), p.383.

36. *ibid.* p.384.

37. *ibid.* p.384, footnote.

38. John Fowles, 'Hardy and the Hag' in *Thomas Hardy After Fifty Years* ed L. St John Butler (London: Macmillan, 1977), p.36.

39. *ibid.* p.41.

40. *ibid.* p.35.

41. G. Rose, '*The French Lieutenant's Woman*: the unconscious significance of a novel to its author' in *American Imago*, 29 (Summer 1972), p.175.

42. John Fowles, 'Notes on an unfinished novel' in *The Novel Today* ed M. Bradbury (London: Fontana, 1982), p.136.

43. M. Bragg, 'Interview with John Fowles' from 'The South Bank Show', London Weekend Television, transcript P/NO 80103, 1982, p.3.

Chapter 5: Escaping the script—the politics of change

1. A. Gorz, *Farewell to the Working Class* (London: Pluto, 1982), p.85.

2. *ibid.* p.85.

3. *ibid.* p.85.

4. S. Benton, 'Adam and Eve' in *New Socialist*, 11 (May–June 1983) p.19.
5. *See* A. Tolson, *The Limits of Masculinity* (London: Tavistock, 1977). In this study, Tolson examines what he sees as a post-war 'crisis' in masculinity among middle-class professional men in terms very similar to those employed by Fowles in *Daniel Martin*. What Tolson calls 'the defensive insecurity of men in post-war society' (p.16), is seen as the result of tensions within contemporary society and capitalism which have undermined the masculine 'presence'. With middle-class men, Tolson argues, the imperialistic, public-school values on which their notions of male identity had been constructed were severely eroded by the experience of two world wars and the intensifying of capitalistic attitudes. Those values, which included an acceptance of hierarchy, duty, privilege, competitiveness, success and emotional repression, have intensified the demands of male roles to a degree that a 'crisis of confidence' (p.86) has set in. Tolson comments: 'At work, the crisis has been met, in typical masculine fashion, by a withdrawal into cynicism covering up a sense of disillusionment.' The young male careerist's experience of the work world 'slowly compromises a man's heroic visions', and the disillusioned professional, trapped in a world he has helped create and from which he benefits in terms of power and money, has only two recourses—either pursue his career with 'overtly cynical calculation' or retreat back 'to the focus of all his patriarchal attitudes: the home and the family' (pp.88-91).

    One point to notice about Tolson's formulation, as he points out, is that 'the alienation of middle-class men, being due less to direct exploitation and more to complex ideological contradictions, is psychological in character. It is, as I have described, a crisis in personal identification.' The point is important, for to talk of a 'crisis' in middle-class masculinity is obviously to beg a lot of questions. Men still wield and benefit from social and economic dominance and privilege. Their experience, therefore, of the contradictions and distortions of the social order from which they benefit is felt, if at all, as a psychological dissatisfaction rather than an economic oppression. It is this that, in Tolson's view, leads the middle-class male to an identity crisis whose resolution is often pursued through sexual relationships (p.100). Of course, Tolson's analysis needs reframing for the 1980s given the experience of unemployment among middle-class men.

6. M. Gussow, 'Talk with John Fowles' in *New York Times Book Review* (13 November 1977), p.84.
7. P. Conradi, *John Fowles* (London: Methuen, 1982), p.95.
8. D. Hall, 'John Fowles's garden' in *Esquire*, 98 (October 1982), p.94.
9. *See* J. Mitchell and J. Rose, *Feminine Sexuality: Jacques Lacan and the École Freudienne* (London: Macmillan, 1982), pp.6, 13, 32, 38. In Juliet Mitchell's words, the castration complex is 'the focal point of the acquisition of culture; it operates as a law whereby men and women

assume their humanity and, inextricably bound up with this, it gives the human meaning of the distinction between the sexes.' (*ibid.* p.13) This 'human meaning' is the organisation of the infant into the category of either male or female and the acquisition of power by the male through a denial of the potential for being 'not male'.

10. *See* A. Tolson, *The Limits of Masculinity* (London: Tavistock, 1977, pp.115-16: Tolson describes the 'socio-sexual *contradiction*' that the 'crisis of middle-class masculinity is counterposed to the emancipation of middle-class women. As insecure careerists, as drop-outs, for the historical reasons I have outlined, middle-class men have been growing more and more dependent on images of domesticity; just as women themselves have been breaking these images apart. And this socio-sexual contradiction has inevitably been experienced, especially by women, as a bitter struggle. Women have only been able to assert their independence at the expense of men, who were, so to speak, moving in the opposite direction.'

11. M. Gussow, 'Talk with John Fowles' in *New York Times Book Review* (13 November 1977), p.3.

12. D. Hall, 'John Fowles's garden' in *Esquire*, 98 (October 1982), p.94.

13. M. Gussow, 'Talk with John Fowles' in *New York Times Book Review* (13 November 1977), p.84.

14. *ibid.* p.3.

15. R.K. Singh, 'An encounter with John Fowles' in *Journal of Modern Literature*, 8, 2 (1980), p.187.

16. M. Gussow, 'Talk with John Fowles' in *New York Times Book Review* (13 November 1977), p.84.

17. John Fowles, 'I write therefore I am' in *Evergreen Review*, 8 (August–September 1964), p.89.

18. John Fowles, 'The Falklands and a death foretold' in *The Guardian* (14 August 1982), p.7.

19. M. Gussow, 'Talk with John Fowles' in *New York Times Book Review* (13 November 1977), p.85.

20. S. Benton, 'Adam and Eve' in *New Socialist*, 11 (May–June 1983), p.18.

21. J. Campbell, 'An interview with John Fowles' in *Contemporary Literature*, 17, 4 (1976), pp.468-9.

22. M. Gussow, 'Talk with John Fowles' in *New York Times Book Review* (13 November 1977), p.85.

23. R. Huffaker, *John Fowles* (Boston, Mass.: G.K. Hall, 1980), p.35.

24. D. Halpern, 'A sort of exile in Lyme Regis' in *London Magazine* (10 March 1971), p.36.

Chapter 6: Men, will they ever grow up?

1. D. Lodge, 'Bibliosexuality' in *The Sunday Times* (10 October 1982).

2. *See* S. Freud, *Jokes and Their Relation to the Unconscious*, ed J. Strachey (Harmondsworth: Penguin, 1981).

3. S. Benton, 'Adam and Eve' in *New Socialist*, 11 (May–June 1983), p.19.

4. D. Halpern, 'A sort of exile in Lyme Regis' in *London Magazine* (10 March 1971), pp.39-40.

5. D. Hall, 'John Fowles's garden' in *Esquire*, 98 (October 1982), p.92.

6. *See* C.G. Jung, *Aion: Researches into the Phenomenology of the Self* (*Collected Works of C.G. Jung*, vol.9, part II), tr. R.F.C. Hull (London: Routledge and Kegan Paul, 1959), pp.12-20.

7. D. Hall, 'John Fowles's garden' in *Esquire*, 98 (October 1982), p.92.

8. S. Benton, 'Adam and Eve' in *New Socialist*, 11 (May–June 1983), p.18.

9. D. Hall, 'John Fowles's garden' in *Esquire*, 98 (October 1982), p.92.

10. S. Benton, 'Adam and Eve' in *New Socialist*, 11 (May–June 1983), p.19.

11. *ibid.* p.19.

12. The term is employed by M. Charney, *Sexual Fiction* (London: Methuen, 1981) as a generic term whose limits are apparent in the absence of any real sexual politics in Charney's arguments.

13. R. Stolley, 'The French Lieutenant's Woman's Man' in *Life*, 29 (May 1970), p.58.

14. *ibid.* p.58.

15. S. Benton, 'Adam and Eve' in *New Socialist*, 11 (May–June 1983), p.19.

16. A. Carter, *The Sadeian Woman* (London: Virago, 1979), p.19.

17. *ibid.* p.17.

18. *ibid.* p.19.

19. See for example J. Seaton, 'Private Lives, Public Display' in *New Socialist*, 8 (November–December 1982), pp.24-5; and, for the replies to Seaton, *New Socialist*, 9 (January–February 1983), pp.5-6, and 10 (March–April, 1983), p.41.

20. B. Brown, 'A feminist interest in pornography: some modest proposals' in *m/f* 5-6 (1981), p.7.

21. *ibid.* pp.6-7.

22. S. Sontag, 'The pornographic imagination' in *The Story of the Eye*, by G. Bataille (Harmondsworth: Penguin, 1982), pp.96, 98.

23. J. Mitchell and J Rose, *Feminine Sexuality: Jacques Lacan and the École Freudienne* (London: Macmillan, 1982), p.47: as Jacqueline Rose puts it, Lacan's view is that within the process of language, 'woman is constructed as an absolute category (excluded and elevated at one and the same time), a category which serves to guarantee that unity [of the subject] on the side of the man. The man places the woman at the basis of his fantasy, or constitutes fantasy through the woman.' It is the 'construction of woman as a category within language' that both differentiates and validates male prerogatives.

24. T. Eagleton, *Literary Theory: An Introduction* (Oxford: Blackwell, 1983), p.48.

25. In his 1977 review of Morris Fraser's *The Death of Narcissus*, Fowles

suggests the significance of the cuckoo-clock motif he later uses in *Mantissa*. Speaking ironically, supposedly on behalf of what he calls the 'mandarin line' of the literary establishment, he berates 'these crude psychiatrist fellows' like Fraser for meddling with the sources of creativity: 'How dare they suggest that dead writers might once have been living, fallible and as crammed with repetitive hang-ups as a room full of cuckoo-clocks?' Fowles himself, on the other hand, finds 'studies like Dr Fraser's worth a ton of traditional criticism', since, because of them, 'We [modern novelists] may know our own cuckoo-clocks or psychic mechanisms better now.' *See* John Fowles, 'For the dark' in *New Statesman*, (18 February 1977), pp.221-2.

26. John Fowles, 'The trouble with starlets' in *Holiday*, 39 (June 1966), p.17.
27. *ibid.* pp.15, 18.
28. *See* John Ellis, 'On Pornography' in *Screen*, 21, 1 (1980), pp.81-108, and Paul Willeman, 'Letter to John' in *Screen*, 21, 2 (1980), pp.53-66.
29. John Fowles, 'The trouble with starlets' in *Holiday*, 39 (June 1966), p.18.
30. E. Wilson, *What Is To Be Done About Violence Against Women?* (Harmondsworth: Penguin, 1983), pp.166.
31. W. Holloway, 'Heterosexual sex: power and desire for the other' in *Sex and Love: New Thoughts on Old Contradictions*, ed Sue Cartledge and Joanna Ryan (London: The Women's Press, 1983), p.136.
32. *ibid.* pp.138-9.
33. E. Wilson, *What Is To Be Done About Violence Against Women?* (Harmondsworth: Penguin, 1983), pp.167-8.

Bibliography

This bibliography lists those works cited in the text and the notes, as well as works which have contributed directly to the development of the arguments in this book.

i Works by John Fowles.

For a full listing up to 1982 see Olshen (1980) and Conradi (1982).

The Aristos. St. Albans: Triad-Granada, 1981.

The Collector. St. Albans: Triad-Panther, 1977.

Daniel Martin. St Albans: Triad-Panther, 1978.

'The demon barber dimension', *The Guardian*, 10 October 1981, p.9.

The Ebony Tower. St. Albans: Granada, 1982.

'The Falklands and a death foretold' *The Guardian*, 14 August 1982, p.7.

'Florentine Fowles', *The Guardian*, 15 March 1983, p.11.

'For the dark', *New Statesman*, 18 February 1977, pp.221-2.

The French Lieutenant's Woman. St Albans: Triad-Panther, 1978.

'Hardy and the Hag', in L. St John Butler (ed.), *Thomas Hardy After Fifty Years*, London: Macmillan, 1977, pp.28-42.

'I write therefore I am', *Evergreen Review*, 8 (August–September 1964), pp.16–17, 89–90.

'Jacqueline Kennedy Onassis and other first (and last) ladies', *Cosmopolitan*, 170 (October 1970), pp.144-49.

The Magus. London: Pan, 1974.

The Magus: A Revised Version. St Albans: Triad-Panther, 1978.

Mantissa. London: Cape, 1982.

'Notes on an unfinished novel', in M. Bradbury (ed.), *The Novel Today*. London: Fontana, 1982, pp.136-50.

'On being English but not British', *The Texas Quarterly* 7 (Autumn 1964), pp.154-62.

Poems. New York: Ecco Press, 1973.

'Seeing nature whole', *Harper's Magazine*, 259 (November 1979), pp.49-68.

'The trouble with starlets', *Holiday*, 39 (June 1966), pp.12-20.

ii   Works about John Fowles.

For a full listing up to 1982 see Olshen (1980) and Conradi (1982).

Benton, Sarah. 'Adam and Eve' (interview), *New Socialist*, 11 (May-June 1983), pp.18-19.

Binns, R. 'A new version of *The Magus*', *Critical Quarterly*, 19, 4 (1977), pp.79-84.

Boston, Richard. 'John Fowles, alone but not lonely', *New York Times Book Review*, 9 November 1969, pp.2, 52-3.

Bragg, Melvyn. 'Interview with John Fowles', South Bank Show, London Weekend Television, P/NO 80103, 1982.

Campbell, James. 'An interview with John Fowles', *Contemporary Literature*, 17, 4 (1976), pp.455-69.

Conradi, Peter. *John Fowles.* London: Methuen, 1982.

Delaney, Frank. 'Interview with John Fowles', Frank Delaney programme, BBC 2, 13 November 1982.

Edwards, L.R. 'Changing our imaginations', *Massachusetts Review*, 11 (Summer 1970), pp.604-8.

Gussow, Mel. 'Talk with John Fowles', *New York Times Book Review*, 13 November 1977, pp.3, 84-5.

Hall, Donald. 'John Fowles's garden' (interview), *Esquire* 98 (October 1982), pp.90-2, 94, 96, 98, 101-2.

Halpern, Daniel. 'A sort of exile in Lyme Regis' (interview), *London Magazine*, 10 March 1971, pp.34-46.

Hieatt, Constance. '*Eliduc* revisited: John Fowles and Marie de France', *English Studies in Canada*, 3 (Fall 1977), pp.351-8.

Huffaker, Robert. *John Fowles.* Boston, Mass.; G.K. Hall, 1980.

Lever, Karen. 'The education of John Fowles', *Critique*, 21 (1979), pp.85-99.

Lodge, David. 'Bibliosexuality', *The Sunday Times*, 10 October 1982.

Mansfield, Elizabeth, 'A sequence of endings: the manuscripts of *The French Lieutenant's Woman*', *Journal of Modern Literature*, 8, 2 (1980-1) pp.275-86.

Newquist, Roy (ed). 'John Fowles' in *Counterpoint*, Chicago, Ill.: Rand McNally, 1964, pp.218-25.

Olshen, Barry. *John Fowles*. New York: Ungar, 1978.

Olshen, Barry and Olshen, Toni. *John Fowles: A Reference Guide*. Boston, Mass.: G.K. Hall, 1980.

Palmer, W.J. *The Fiction of John Fowles: Tradition, Art and the Loneliness of Selfhood*. Columbia, Mo.: University of Missouri Press, 1974.

Robinson, Robert. 'Giving the reader a choice—a conversation with John Fowles', *The Listener*, 31 October 1974, p.584.

Rose, Gilbert. '*The French Lieutenant's Woman*: the unconscious significance of a novel to its author', *American Imago*, 29 (Summer 1972), pp.165-76.

Sage, Lorna. 'John Fowles' (interview), *The New Review*, 1 October 1974, pp.31-7.

'Of small importance', *The Guardian*, 7 October 1982, p.10.

Singh, Raman K. 'An encounter with John Fowles', *Journal of Modern Literature*, 8, 2, (1980), pp.181-202.

Stolley, Richard. 'The French Lieutenant's Woman's man', *Life*, 29 (May 1970), pp.56-60.

Wolfe, Peter. *John Fowles, Magus and Moralist*. London: Associated University Press, 1976.

iii Works on masculinity, gender and theories of sexuality

Abel, E. (ed). *Writing and Sexual Difference*. Brighton: Harvester, 1983.

Allen, Sandra (*et al.*), *Conditions of Illusion: Papers from the Women's Movement*. Leeds: Feminist Books, 1974.

Barker-Benfield, G.J. *The Horrors of the Half-Known Life: Male Attitudes Towards Women and Sexuality in Nineteenth Century America*. New York: Harper and Row, 1976.

Barrett, M. *Women's Oppression Today: Problems in Marxist Feminist Analysis*. London: Verso, 1980.

Barrett, M. and McIntosh, M. *The Anti-Social Family*. London: Verso/New Left Books, 1982.

Benjamin, J. 'The bonds of love: rational violence and erotic domination', *Feminist Studies*, 6 (1980), pp.144-74.

Bettelheim, Bruno. *Symbolic Wounds: Puberty Rites and the Envious Male*. London: Thames and Hudson, 1955.

Brown, Beverley. 'A feminist interest in pornography: some modest proposals', *m/f*, 5-6 (1981), pp.5-18.

Brunt, R. and Rowan, C. *Feminism, Culture and Politics*. London: Lawrence and Wishart, 1982.

Campbell, Beatrix. 'Sexuality and submission', in Allen (1974).

Campioni, Mia and Gross, Liz. 'Little Hans: the production of Oedipus', in P. Foss and M. Morris (eds), *Language, Sexuality and Subversion*. Darlington, New South Wales: Feral Publications, 1978.

Carlton, Eric. *Sexual Anxiety: A Study of Male Impotence*. Oxford: Martin Robertson, 1980.

Cartledge, Sue and Ryan, Joanna *Sex and Love: New Thoughts on Olu Contradictions*. London: The Women's Press, 1983.

Carter. Angela. *The Sadeian Woman*. London: Virago, 1979.

'Victims of machismo', *The Guardian*, 2 September 1982, p.8.

Charney, Maurice. *Sexual Fiction*. London: Methuen, 1981.

Chesler, Phyllis. *About Men*. London: The Women's Press, 1978.

Chodorov, Nancy. *The Reproduction of Mothering*. London: University of California Press, 1978.

Cockburn, C. *Brothers: Male Dominance and Technological Change*. London: Pluto, 1983.

Comfort, Alex. *The Anxiety Makers*. London: Nelson, 1967.

Coote, Anna and Campbell, Beatrix. *Sweet Freedom*. London: Pan, 1982.

Coser, R.L. 'The principle of patriarchy: The case of *The Magic Flute*', *Signs*, 4, 2 (1978), pp.337-48.

Coward, Rosalind. *Patriarchal Precedents: Sexuality and Social Relations*. London: Routledge and Kegan Paul, 1983.

'The making of the feminine', in M. Hoyles (ed), *Changing Childhood*. London: Readers and Writers, 1979.

Dworkin, Andrea. *Pornography: Men Possessing Women*. London: The Women's Press, 1981.

Eardley, Tony, Humphries, Martin, and Morrison, Paul. *About Men*. London: Broadcasting Support Services, 1983. Booklet to accompany three films made by Kestrel Films for Channel 4, which were first shown September 1983 and are available from Concord Films Council, Suffolk.

Easlea, Brian. *Fathering the Unthinkable: Masculinity, Scientists and the Nuclear Arms Race*. London: Pluto, 1983.

Science and Sexual Oppression: Patriarchy's Confrontation With Women and Nature. London: Weidenfeld and Nicolson, 1981.

Ehrenreich, Barbara. *The Hearts of Men*. London: Pluto, 1983.

Ellis, John. 'On pornography', *Screen*, 21, 1 (1980), pp.81-108.

Farrell, Warren. *The Liberated Man*. New York: Bantam, 1979.

Fasteau, Marc Feigen. *The Male Machine*. New York: McGraw Hill,

1974.

Faust, Beatrice. *Women, Sex and Pornography.* Harmondsworth: Penguin, 1982.

Feminist Review, 'Sexuality Issue' 11 (Summer 1982).

Foucault, Michel. *The History of Sexuality.* Vol. I, *An Introduction,* tr. R. Hurley. Harmondsworth: Penguin, 1981.

Frankl, George. *The Failure of the Sexual Revolution.* London: New English Library, 1975.

Freud, Sigmund. *Introductory Lectures on Psychoanalysis,* ed J. Strachey. Harmondsworth: Penguin, 1975.

    Jokes and Their Relation to the Unconscious, ed. J. Strachey. Harmondsworth: Penguin, 1981.

    New Introductory Lectures on Psychoanalysis. ed J. Strachey. Harmondsworth: Penguin, 1981.

    On Sexuality, ed. A. Richards. Harmondsworth: Penguin, 1977.

Friedman, Scarlet, and Sarah, Elizabeth (eds). *On the Problem of Men.* London: The Women's Press, 1982.

Gallop, Jane. *Feminism and Psychoanalysis: The Daughter's Seduction.* London: Macmillan, 1982.

Griffin, Susan. *Pornography and Silence.* London: The Women's Press, 1982.

Habegger, A. *Gender, Fantasy and Realism in American Literature.* New York: Columbia University Press, 1982.

Harrison, Brian. *Separate Spheres.* London: Croom Helm, 1978.

Harrison, Fraser. *The Dark Angel: Aspects of Victorian Sexuality.* London: Fontana, 1979.

Harrison, J.B. 'Men's roles and men's lives', *Signs,* 4, 2 (1978), pp.324-36.

Hays, H.R. *The Dangerous Sex: The Myth of Feminine Evil.* London: Methuen, 1968.

Heath, Stephen. *The Sexual Fix.* London: Macmillan, 1982.

Hoch, Paul. *White Hero Black Beast: Racism, Sexism and the Mask of Masculinity.* London: Pluto, 1979.

Holloway, Wendy. '"I just wanted to kill a woman." Why? The Ripper and male sexuality', *Feminist Review,* 9 (Autumn 1981), pp.33-40.

Illich, Ivan. *Gender.* London: Marion Boyes, 1983.

Jung, C.G. *Aion: Researches into the Phenomenology of the Self,* tr. R.F.C.

BIBLIOGRAPHY

Hull. London: Routledge and Kegan Paul, 1959.

The Development of Personality, tr. R.F.C. Hull. London: Routledge and Kegan Paul, 1954.

C.G. Jung Speaking: Interviews and Encounters, ed W. McGuire and R.F.C. Hull. London: Thames and Hudson, 1978.

Kuhn, A. and Wolpe, A.M. *Feminism and Materialism*. London: Routledge and Kegan Paul, 1978.

Mitchell, Juliet. *Psychoanalysis and Feminism*. Harmondsworth: Penguin, 1982.

Mitchell, Juliet, and Rose, Jacqueline (eds). *Feminine Sexuality: Jacques Lacan and the École Freudienne*. London: Macmillan, 1982.

Myers, Kathy. 'The new women's question: power, patriarchy and privilege', *New Socialist*, 11 (May–June 1983), pp.14-17.

Oakley, Ann. *Sex, Gender and Society*. London: Temple Smith, 1972.

Phillips, Eileen. *The Left and the Erotic*. London: Lawrence and Wishart, 1983.

Plech, J.H. and Sawyer, J. (eds). *Men and Masculinity*. New Jersey: Prentice Hall, 1974.

Red Collective. *The Politics of Sexuality in Capitalism*. London: Red Collective/Publications Distribution Collective, 1978.

Reynaud, Emmanuel. *Holy Virility: The Social Construction of Masculinity*. London: Pluto, 1983.

Seaton, Jean. 'Private lives, public display', *New Socialist*, 8 (November–December 1982), pp.24-5. See also *New Socialist* 9 (January–February 1983), pp.5-6, and 10 (March–April 1983) p.41 for replies to Seaton.

Shaw, E. *Strategies of Being Female*. Brighton: Harvester, 1983.

Sontag, Susan. 'The pornographic imagination' in Georges Bataille, *The Story of the Eye*. Harmondsworth: Penguin, 1982.

Tannahill, Reay. *Sex in History*. London: Hamish Hamilton, 1980.

Todd, Janet. *Gender and Literary Voice*. New York: Holmes and Meier, 1980.

Tolson, Andrew. *The Limits of Masculinity*. London: Tavistock, 1977.

Trudgill, Eric. *Madonnas and Magdalens*. New York: Holmes and Meier, 1976.

Turkle, Shelley. *Psychoanalytic Politics: Jacques Lacan and Freud's French Revolution*. London: Burnett-Deutsch, 1979.

Weeks, Jeffrey. *Sex, Politics and Society*. London: Longmans, 1981.

Willeman, Paul. 'Letter to John', *Screen*, 21, 2 (1980), pp.53-66.

Wilson, Elizabeth. *What Is To Be Done About Violence Against Women?* Harmondsworth: Penguin, 1983.

Zilbergeld, Bernard. *Men and London: Fontana, 1980.*

iv Other Works

Alain-Fournier. *Le Grand Meaulnes.* Harmondsworth: Penguin, 1983.

Barthes, Roland. *Mythologies.* St. Albans: Granada, 1979.

Barthes, Roland. *The Pleasure of the Text,* tr. Richard Miller. New York: Hill and Wang, 1975.

Brown, Beverley. 'Private faces in public places', in *Ideology and Consciousness,* 7, pp.3-16.

Colman, Marshall. *Continuous Excursions: Politics and Personal Life.* London: Pluto, 1982.

Coward, Rosalind, and Ellis, John. *Language and Materialism.* London: Routledge and Kegan Paul, 1977.

Culler, Jonathan. *On Deconstruction.* London: Routledge and Kegan Paul, 1983.

Derrida, Jacques. *Spurs: Nietzche's Style.* London: University of Chicago Press, 1979.

Eagleton, Terry. *Literary Theory: An Introduction.* Oxford: Blackwell, 1983.

The Rape of Clarissa. Oxford: Blackwell, 1982.

Fairbairns, Zoë. *Stand We At Last.* London: Virago, 1983.

Frye, Northrop. *The Secular Scripture.* Cambridge Mass.: Harvard, 1976.

Gorz, André. *Farewell to the Working Class.* London: Pluto, 1982.

Gramsci, Antonio. *Selections from The Prison Notebooks,* tr. and ed Quentin Hoare and Geoffrey Nowell Smith. London: Lawrence and Wishart, 1978.

Grass, Günther. *The Flounder.* Harmondsworth: Penguin, 1979.

Kundera, Milan. *Laughable Lovès,* tr. Suzanne Rappaport. Harmondsworth: Penguin, 1981.

Marx, Karl. *The Portable Marx,* ed. Eugene Kamenka. London: Viking-Penguin, 1983.

McEwan, Ian. *In Between The Sheets.* London: Pan, 1979.

Sachs, Hans. *The Creative Unconscious.* Cambridge Mass.: Sci-Aut, 1951.

Simon, Roger. *Gramsci's Political Thought: An Introduction.* London: Lawrence and Wishart, 1982.

Stevenson, R.L. *Dr Jekyll and Mr Hyde.* London: Collins, 1958.

Name Index

Subject Index